T0125046

best | designed

Martin Nicholas Kunz

wellness hotels

WESTERN AND CENTRAL EUROPE . THE ALPS . THE MEDITERRANEAN
WEST- UND MITTELEUROPA . ALPEN . MITTELMEER

Second updated edition
2. aktualisierte Auflage

avedition

Langenlois
Donaueschingen
Bezau
Zell am See
Weggis
Ischgl
Interlaken
Lana
Arosa
Zermatt
Vals
Geneva
Verona
Milan
Helsinki
Cowley
Chandler's Cross
Berlin
Hagetmau
Split
Barcelona
Tarragona
Corsica
Mallorca
Athens
Antalya/Belek
Mykonos
Bodrum
Crete
Paphos
Madeira

"Knowest thou the land where the lemon trees bloom?"... Since Goethe wrote this poem, it has become a symbol of the longing for foreign countries and an escape from everyday life. Anyone reading these melodious lines dreams of Mediterranean landscapes with olive trees and cypresses, fragrant herbs and full-bodied wines, ancient art and culture that are thousands of years old—in short: of a new awareness of life, of wellness for all the senses. Italy, the realm of dolce vita, is a destination that allows such dreams to come true. But it is not the only one. Islands like Cypress with its beaches where Aphrodite rose out of the water, Corsica with its incomparably clear light, or Majorca with its fincas that put a definitive end to all of the horror stories about how it has become Germany's seventeenth state—these are places where you can feel good in every way, where body and soul come into harmony. And the finest oases can be found even in the cool heart of a Scandinavian metropolis, in the green landscapes of England, or in the rugged world of the Swiss mountains. This is because hoteliers in all of these places have realized that "wellness" means more than a bathrobe in the room, a low-calorie meal on the menu, and a massage table under neon light. Here is where architects have harmoniously fit their buildings into the surrounding environment or designed them in an inspiring contrast to it; and it is here that interior designers have proved their strong sense of style and taste.

03 04

Thanks to major names like Bulgari, Sir Rocco Forte, Graft, Mario Botta, or Matteo Thun, Europe has considerably shortened the distance to Asia and the Indian Ocean in terms of wellness hotels. But also "little," unknown designers participate in this race to catch up: Many of them come directly from the region or country in which a new hotel is constructed, let the attachment to their homeland flow into their designs, and give each building an individual face of its own. The period in which the European wellness hotels were nothing more than somewhat desperate and unimaginative copies of exotic dream spas is over. Spain has no reason to hide behind the Seychelles, a house in Turkey can be just as enchanting as one in Thailand, and Italy's landscapes fascinate with as much beauty as the Indian Ocean. It doesn't always have to be the fragrance of ylang ylang or frangipani that lets you take a deep breath—sometimes even the fruity-fresh aroma of a lemon is enough.

Anna Streubert

01 | The Omnia

02 | Blue Palace Resort & Spa

03 | Tschuggen Grand Hotel

04 | Therme Vals

05 06

„Kennst Du das Land, wo die Zitronen blühn?" … Seit Goethe dieses Gedicht schrieb, ist es zum Symbol für die Sehnsucht nach fremden Ländern und den Ausbruch aus dem Alltag geworden. Wer die klangvollen Zeilen liest, träumt von mediterranen Landschaften mit Olivenbäumen und Zypressen, von duftenden Kräutern und vollmundigen Weinen, von Jahrtausende alter Kunst und Kultur – kurz: von einem neuen Lebensgefühl, von Wellness für alle Sinne. Italien, das Reich des dolce vita, ist ein Ziel, das solche Träume Wirklichkeit werden lässt – aber nicht das einzige. Auch Inseln wie Zypern mit seinen Stränden, an denen Aphrodite aus dem Wasser stieg, Korsika mit seinem unvergleichlich klaren Licht oder Mallorca mit seinen Fincas, die allen Schauergeschichten vom siebzehnten deutschen Bundesland ein definitives Ende bereiten, sind Orte, an denen man sich rundum wohl fühlt; wo Körper und Seele in Einklang kommen. Und auch im kühlen Herzen einer skandinavischen Metropole, in den grünen Landschaften Englands oder in der rauen Schweizer Bergwelt gibt es Oasen vom Feinsten. Denn überall dort haben Hoteliers erkannt, dass „Wellness" mehr bedeutet als ein Bademantel im Zimmer, ein kalorienarmes Menü auf der Karte und eine Massagebank unter Neonlicht. Überall dort haben Architekten ihre Bauten harmonisch in die Umgebung eingepasst oder in inspirierendem Kontrast zu ihr gestaltet, und überall dort haben Interieurdesigner Stilsicherheit und Geschmack bewiesen. Dank

großer Namen wie Bulgari, Sir Rocco Forte, Graft, Mario Botta oder Matteo Thun hat Europa den Abstand zu Asien und zum Indischen Ozean deutlich verkürzt, was Wellnesshotels betrifft. Aber auch „kleine", unbekannte Designer sind an dieser Aufholjagd beteiligt: Viele von ihnen stammen direkt aus der Region oder dem Land, in dem ein neues Hotel entsteht, lassen die Verbundenheit mit ihrer Heimat in ihre Entwürfe einfließen und verleihen jedem Bau ein eigenes, individuelles Gesicht. Die Zeit, in der europäische Wellnesshotels nichts anderes waren als einigermaßen verzweifelte und fantasielose Kopien exotischer Traum-Spas, ist vorbei. Spanien hat keinen Grund, sich hinter den Seychellen zu verstecken, ein Haus in der Türkei kann so zauberhaft sein wie eines in Thailand, in Italiens Landschaften faszinieren so viele Schönheiten wie im Indischen Ozean. Es muss ja nicht immer der Duft nach Ylang Ylang oder Frangipani sein, der uns aufatmen lässt – manchmal genügt schon das fruchtig-frische Aroma einer Zitrone.

Anna Streubert

05 | Adam & Eve

06 | EV

07 | Byblos Art Hotel Villa Amista

08 | Estalagem da Ponta do Sol

choupana hills resort & spa | madeira . portugal

DESIGN: Michel de Camaret, Didier Lefort

High up on an exposed plateau above the island capital of Funchal lies this new type of resort and wellness hotel with 34 elegantly designed pile buildings. The architecture focuses on harmony as Asiatic forms and international modernity combine with Portuguese tradition. In addition, the architecture group with the Frenchmen Michel de Camaret and Didier Lefort already emphasized an ecological concept in the early planning phase to integrate the subtropical vegetation as a solid component into the complex. The design of the interiors, decoration, and furnishings of these mini-villas is closely linked with the outside facilities. The individual villas are divided into two 132 square feet units with a living and sleeping room, as well as an airy bath that is filled with daylight. Two ceiling-high sliding glass doors connect the interior seamlessly with the large timber-floor terrace. The panorama view above Funchal and the ocean far below is sensational. The heart of the facility is an extensive health, beauty, and wellness program. Massages, aromatherapies, sauna, a Turkish hammam, facial and body treatments, as well as coordinated dietary plans ensure individually designed relaxation.

Hoch oben auf einem exponierten Plateau über der Inselhauptstadt Funchal liegt dieses neuartige Resort- und Wellnesshotel mit 34 elegant gestalteten Pfahlbauten. Die Architektur ist auf Harmonie bedacht, obgleich sich in die portugiesische Tradition asiatische Formen und internationale Modernität mischen. Zudem setzte die Architektengruppe mit den Franzosen Michel de Camaret und Didier Lefort schon in der frühen Planungsphase auf ein ökologisches Konzept, das die subtropische Vegetation als festen Bestandteil in die Anlage einbinden sollte. Die Gestaltung der Innenräume, die Dekoration und die Möblierung dieser Mini-Villen sind eng mit den Außenanlagen verknüpft. Die einzelnen Villen teilen sich in zwei 40 Quadratmeter große Einheiten mit Wohn- und Schlafraum sowie luftigem, tageslichtdurchflutetem Bad. Zwei raumhohe Glasschiebetüren verbinden den Innenraum nahtlos mit der großen Holzdielenterrasse. Sensationell ist von dort die Panoramaaussicht über Funchal und den tief unten liegenden Ozean. Kern der Anlage ist ein umfangreiches Gesundheits-, Schönheits- und Wohlfühlangebot. Massagen, Aromatherapien, Sauna, türkisches Hammam, Gesichts- und Körperbehandlungen sowie abgestimmte Ernährungspläne sorgen für eine individuell gestaltete Entspannung.

01 | The Choupana Hills Resort & Spa lies high above the hills of Funchal.

Hoch oben über den Hügeln von Funchal liegt das Choupana Hills Resort & Spa.

02
03
04

02 | The lounge is a cozy hall that looks very inviting.

Ein gemütlicher Saal zum Verweilen ist die Lounge.

03 | The Bedrooms promise relaxation.

Die Schlafzimmer versprechen Entspannung.

04 | The interior rooms have an exotic and purist design.

Die Innenräume sind exotisch und puristisch zugleich gestaltet.

05 | The heart of the hotel is the pool in the spa area.

Herz des Hotels ist der Pool im Spa-Bereich.

05

estalagem da ponta do sol | madeira . portugal

DESIGN: Tiago Oliveira, Carvalho Araujo

A more spectacular location for a hotel can hardly be imagined: All of the hotel buildings are spread across ridges of a cliff that juts into the ocean. Even the two-story main building with the reception, lobby, bar, and clubroom stands high above the fishing village of Ponta do Sol. It is surrounded by a roofed terrace and park-like garden with mature trees and palms. The young Portuguese architect Tiago Oliveira and the designer Carvalho Araujo have positioned an esthetic highlight one cliff plateau higher: the restaurant. The building is a simple, white cube with glass from floor-to-ceiling and a muted décor. This geometric clarity and the abstention from purely ornamental decoration in particular create an apparent harmony with the precipitous cliff landscape. A staircase or elevator from the restaurant takes guests to the 54 rooms, which are distributed among three buildings. The walls are primarily kept in white and furnishings are reduced. All of the rooms have their own balcony or a terrace that has a view either of Ponta do Sol, hills and ocean, or directly over the cliff toward the east. One of the most beautiful views is from the swimming pool, which looks like it blends directly into the ocean.

Eine spektakulärere Lage für ein Hotel kann man sich kaum vorstellen: alle Hotelgebäude verteilen sich auf einem in den Ozean hineinragenden Felsausläufer. Schon das zweigeschossige Hauptgebäude mit Empfang, Lobby, Bar und Clubraum steht erhaben über dem Fischerdorf Ponta do Sol. Umgeben ist es von einer überdachten Terrasse und einem parkähnlichen Garten mit altem Baumbestand und Palmen. Ein Felsplateau höher haben der junge portugiesische Architekt Tiago Oliveira und der Designer Carvalho Araujo ein ästhetisches Highlight plaziert: das Restaurant. Das Gebäude ist ein schlichter, weißer Kubus mit raumhoher Verglasung und zurückhaltender Innenausstattung. Gerade diese geometrische Klarheit und der Verzicht auf nur schmückende Dekoration schafft eine augenscheinliche Harmonie mit der schroffen Felslandschaft. Vom Restaurant gelangt man über einen Treppenaufgang oder mit einem Aufzug zu den 54 Gästezimmern, die auf drei Gebäude verteilt sind. Die Wände sind vorwiegend in weiß gehalten, die Möblierung ist reduziert. Alle Zimmer haben einen eigenen Balkon oder eine Terrasse, entweder mit Blick auf Ponta do Sol, Hügel und Ozean oder direkt über der Klippe in Richtung Osten. Eine der schönsten Aussichten hat man vom Schwimmbad aus, das direkt in den Ozean überzugehen scheint.

01 | The restaurant with its simple design offers a breathtaking view.

Einen atemberaubenden Blick genießt man vom schlicht gestalteten Restaurant.

02 | A spot between the sky and the earth – the terrace.

Ein Platz zwischen Himmel und Erde – die Terrasse.

03 | Architecture and nature are combined into a harmonious unity in Estalagem da Ponta do Sol.

Architektur und Natur werden im Estalagem da Ponta do Sol zu einer harmonischen Einheit verknüpft.

04 | One of the rooms above the cliff. If you leave the balcony door open, you will only hear the rushing of waves and screeching of seagulls.

Eines der Zimmer über den Klippen. Wer die Balkontür offen lässt, hört nur noch das Rauschen der Wellen und das Geschrei der Möwen.

05 | The pool offers not only a fascinating view of the ocean, but also of the mountains along the southern coast of Madeira.

Vom Pool bietet sich nicht nur eine faszinierende Aussicht auf das Meer, sondern auch auf die Berge entlang der Südküste Madeiras.

h 1898 | barcelona . spain

DESIGN: Rosa Roselló

This establishment is sheer prestige: The H 1898 stands proudly on La Rambla and reveals a fantastic view across Barcelona from the roof terrace with its pool. When you stand up here for the first time, you will almost be tempted to set up your quarters under the open sky and just look in astonishment for days and nights on end—but then you would miss out on one of the most beautiful interiors of the city. The building was originally constructed at the end of the 19th century as the headquarters of the Compañía of General de Tabacos de Filipinas—its colonial atmosphere is still tangible today and coupled with modern design in a sophisticated manner. Dark parquet that has been highly polished and austere lines lend the 169 rooms and suites a very elegant atmosphere; and the black-and-white photography—for which Maria Espeus made a special trip to the Philippines—gives the ambience its finishing touches. The Suites Coloniales with their private pool and garden are a hot tip—so much Mediterranean luxury at the center of a metropolis is unique (the same also applies to the pool in the vaulted cellar!). For dinner, people meet at the restaurant with its minimalist style and then let the day come to an end where it began so perfectly: on the roof terrace.

Diese Adresse ist Prestige pur: Das H 1898 thront direkt an „La Rambla“ und eröffnet von der Dachterrasse mit Pool aus einen fantastischen Blick über Barcelona. Wer zum ersten Mal hier oben steht, ist fast versucht, sein Quartier unter freiem Himmel aufzuschlagen und tage- und nächtelang nur zu schauen und zu staunen – doch dann entginge ihm eines der schönsten Interieurs der Stadt. Ursprünglich wurde das Gebäude Ende des 19. Jahrhunderts als Sitz der Compañía General de Tabacos de Filipinas erbaut – seine koloniale Atmosphäre ist noch heute spürbar und wird raffiniert mit modernem Design verbunden. Dunkles, auf Hochglanz poliertes Parkett und strenge Linien verleihen den 169 Zimmern und Suiten etwas sehr Elegantes; und die Schwarz-Weiß-Fotografien, für die Maria Espeus extra auf die Philippinen reiste, geben dem Ambiente den letzten Schliff. Ein Geheimtipp sind die „Suites Coloniales“ mit privatem Pool und Garten – so viel mediterraner Luxus mitten in einer Metropole ist einzigartig (gleiches gilt übrigens für den Pool im Gewölbekeller!). Zum Dinner trifft man sich im minimalistisch gehaltenen Restaurant und lässt den Tag anschließend dort ausklingen, wo er so perfekt begonnen hat: auf der Dachterrasse.

01 | So close to the sky: The roof terrace with its outdoor pool.

Dem Himmel so nah: Die Dachterrasse mit Outdoor-Pool.

02 | Swimming on the historic paths: The indoor pool.

Auf historischen Spuren schwimmen: Der Indoor-Pool.

03 | Exotic and elegant: The clearly designed rooms.
Exotisch und elegant: Die klar designten Zimmer.

04 | Cultivated colonial style: Homage to the past.

Gepflegter Kolonialstil: Hommage an die Vergangenheit.

05 | Hot spot: The bar, one of the trendy places on La Rambla.

Hot spot: Die Bar, eines der In-Lokale an „La Rambla".

06 | Great architect: The building was designed by Josep Oriol Mestres.

Großer Architekt: Der Bau stammt von Josep Oriol Mestres.

07 | Green oasis: Some Suites offer a pool and garden.

Grüne Oase: Einige Suiten bieten einen Pool und Garten.

le méridien ra beach hotel & spa | tarragona . spain

DESIGN: Espinet i Ubach Arquitectes

The Hotel Le Méridien RA Beach Hotel & Spa is just outside of Barcelona. The manorial estate was already built in 1929 by the Sant Joan Order in the breathtaking landscape of Costa Dourada in Catalonia. The spired walls and the interior of the futuristic additions now conceal uncompromising modernity. The esthetic interplay is a success: the minimalist lobby lies under whitewashed archways and ceiling-high windows reveal the view of the golden beach Sant Salvador and the Mediterranean coast in all directions. The water also plays a major role in the 23,600 square feet wellness realm with its pool landscape. Seawater with a very high iodine concentration because of the offshore algae banks is used for the thalasso therapies. In the luxurious La Prairie huts, guests can enjoy the famous Swiss treatments ranging from the classic mud pack to massages to acupuncture and dietary advice. For the sundowner, people meet at the piano bar of the order's former chapel—or stay completely relaxed in the hammocks of the private beach club.

Vor den Toren Barcelonas liegt das Hotel Le Méridien RA Beach Hotel & Spa. Bereits 1929 erbaute der Sant Joan Orden das herrschaftliche Anwesen in die atemberaubende Landschaft der Costa Dourada in Katalonien. Heute verbirgt sich hinter den zinnenbesetzten Mauern und in den futuristischen Anbauten kompromisslose Moderne. Das ästhetische Wechselspiel ist gelungen: die minimalistische Lobby liegt unter weißgetünchten Bogengängen und raumhohe Fenster geben überall den Blick auf den goldenen Strand Sant Salvador und die Mittelmeerküste frei. Das Wasser spielt auch in dem 7200 Quadratmeter großen Wellness-Reich mit Poollandschaft eine zentrale Rolle. Bei den Thalassotherapien wird Meerwasser verwendet, das durch eine vorgelagerte Algenbank eine sehr hohe Jodkonzentration aufweist. In den luxuriösen La-Prairie-Hütten können Gäste die berühmten Schweizer Behandlungen genießen, von der klassischen Schlammpackung über Massagen bis hin zur Akupunktur und Ernährungsberatung. Zum Sundowner trifft man sich an der Piano-Bar in der früheren Ordenskapelle – oder ganz entspannt in den Hängematten des privaten Beach Clubs.

01 | Peacefully letting your thoughts drift is the law of the evening hour.

In Ruhe in die Ferne schweifen ist das Gesetz der Abendstunde.

02

02 | Stylish comfort in the aristocratic-reduced design.

Stilvolle Gemütlichkeit in edel-reduziertem Design.

03 | Even when the evenings are cool, you can still look up at the starry sky in the protected winter garden.

Selbst an kühlen Abenden kann man im geschützen Wintergarten in den Sternenhimmel schauen.

04 | The view from the sundeck extends over the tops of the palm trees to the ocean.

Vom Sonnendeck reicht der Blick über die Palmenwipfel bis aufs Meer hinaus.

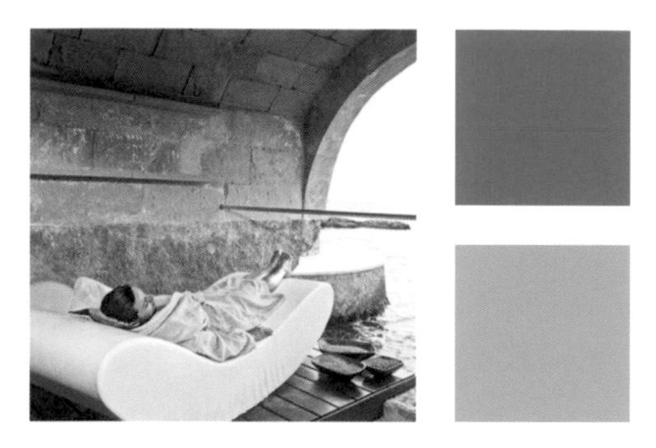

hotel maricel | mallorca . spain

DESIGN: Hospes Design

During the 1940s, a businessman had this palatial villa built for the high society. A square tower with an elongated side wing of terraces and extensions was built for this purpose. In turn, these have numerous columns and elegantly sweeping arcades running through them on several levels. The plateau explains the name of the complex—Maricel is composed of the Spanish words for sea and sky, an allusion to the merging of the elements here. The hotel's pool actually extends out to the ocean on this plateau. The gentle waves of the open sea start immediately beyond its flat edge. Transitions that appear to be flowing—this is how the style of Maricel can be described on the whole. The young architecture of the Hospes Design Team is considerately integrated into the manorial architecture. The freestanding bathtubs are also reminiscent of earlier times. However, the 29 double rooms and suites are otherwise dominated by modern influences. Clear forms and colors determine the furniture; behind the timber ceilings gleams light that cuts the shadows into strips. Veranda zones with rattan furniture and radiant white pillows await a select audience in front of the large windows.

In den vierziger Jahren ließ ein Geschäftsmann diese palastartige Villa für die noble Gesellschaft errichten. Dafür wurde ein quadratischer Turmbau mit gestrecktem Seitenflügel von Terrassen und Anbauten umsäumt. Diese sind wiederum auf mehreren Ebenen von zahlreichen Säulen und elegant geschwungenen Arkaden durchzogen. Auf einem Plateau erklärt sich der Name der Anlage – „Maricel" setzt sich aus den spanischen Wörtern für Meer und Himmel zusammen und spielt auf die Verschmelzung der Elemente an. Denn auf eben diesem Plateau ragt der Pool des Hauses zum Meer hinaus. Hinter der flachen Kante beginnen sofort die sanften Wellen der offenen See. Übergänge, die zu fließen scheinen – so ließe sich insgesamt der Stil vom Maricel beschreiben. Schonend integriert sich die junge Architektur des Hospes Design Teams in die herrschaftliche Architektur. An frühere Zeiten erinnern auch die frei stehenden Badewannen. Sonst dominieren in den 29 Doppelzimmern und Suiten allerdings moderne Einflüsse. Klare Formen und Farben bestimmen das Mobiliar; hinter dielenartigen Decken glimmt Licht, das den Schatten in Streifen schneidet. Vor den großen Fenstern warten Verandazonen mit Rattanmöbeln und strahlend weißen Kissen auf ein ausgesuchtes Publikum.

01 | The tower offers a beautiful view of the pool with its overflow basin that leads directly to the sea.

Vom Turm aus hat man eine schöne Sicht auf den Pool mit seinem Überlaufbecken direkt ins Meer.

02 | The stylish cocktail bar also attracts the locals.

Die stilvolle Cocktailbar zieht auch Einheimische an.

03 | Clear forms, raw materials, and well-chosen interiors distinguish the rooms.

Klare Formen, rohe Materialien und ein ausgewähltes Interieur zeichnen die Zimmer aus.

04 | The majestic palace from the 1940s only has 29 rooms.

Der majestätische Palast aus den vierziger Jahren besitzt nur 29 Zimmer.

05 | Simple ionic columns frame the picturesque views.

Schlichte ionische Säulen umrahmen malerische Aussichten.

06 | The comfortable loungers on the terrace provide relaxation.

Entspannung bringen die bequemen Liegen auf der Terrasse.

06

son brull hotel & spa | mallorca . spain

DESIGN: Sebastian Gamundí, Ignasi Forteza

A trip to Son Brull is a journey into Majorca's past because the history of this estate extends back to the 12th century. An Arabian Alquería (a type of farmhouse) was originally built here at the foot of Puig de Maria in the north of the island. It was later used by the Desbrull family as a private residence. In the 18th century, it was transformed into a Jesuit monastery, and then back into a farm again. Son Brull now belongs to the legendary hoteliers Suau—they combine tradition and the modern spirit, the Mediterranean art of living, and urban chic, wellness, and culinary delights so skillfully that Relais & Châteaux accepted the establishment as a member. The raw charm of Majorca is present everywhere in Son Brull: For example, the local designer Ignasi Forteza has created the 23 rooms and suites in a purist style, the bar was set up in a former olive press, and Majorcan cuisine is on the menu of the Restaurant 3165—which, incidentally, owes its name to the local saying that Son Brull is "the house of 365 windows." The spa uses native products such as rosemary, honey, or almond oil for skin care. From the king-size loungers at the pool, you can look far out across the island—welcome to an homage to Majorca.

Eine Reise nach Son Brull ist eine Reise in die Vergangenheit Mallorcas – denn die Geschichte dieses Anwesens reicht bis ins 12. Jahrhundert zurück. Damals entstand hier, am Fuß des Puig de Maria im Norden der Insel, eine arabische „Alquería“ (eine Art Bauernhof). Sie wurde später von der Familie Desbrull als Privatwohnsitz genutzt, im 18. Jahrhundert in ein Jesuitenkloster und schließlich wieder in eine Farm verwandelt. Heute ist Son Brull im Besitz der legendären Hoteliers Suau – sie verbinden Tradition und Moderne, mediterrane Lebenskunst und urbanen Chic, Wellness und Kulinarik so gekonnt, dass „Relais & Châteaux“ das Haus als Mitglied aufnahm. Der raue Charme Mallorcas ist in Son Brull überall präsent: So hat der einheimische Designer Ignasi Forteza die 23 Zimmer und Suiten puristisch gestaltet, die Bar wurde in einer ehemaligen Olivenpresse eingerichtet, und im Restaurant 3165 stehen mallorquinische Menüs auf der Karte - seinen Namen verdankt das Lokal übrigens dem Sprichwort, Son Brull sei „das Haus der 365 Fenster“. Im Spa pflegen lokale Produkte wie Rosmarin, Honig oder Mandelöl, und von den Kingsize-Liegen am Pool aus blickt man weit über die Insel – willkommen zu einer Hommage an Mallorca.

01 | Chill out: The day beds measure a wonderful 6.5 x 6.5 feet.
Chill out: Die Tagesbetten messen traumhafte 2 x 2 Meter.

02 | Everything flows: The indoor-outdoor pool has a simple design.

Alles fließt: Der Indoor-Outdoor-Pool ist schlicht designt.

03 | Very artistic: All of the pictures come from Majorcan painters.

Kunstvoll: Alle Bilder stammen von mallorquinischen Malern.

04 | Avantgarde: The rooms and suites offer state-of-the art technology.

Avantgarde: Die Zimmer und Suiten bieten modernste Technik.

casadelmar | corsica . france

DESIGN: Jean François Bodin, Carole Marcellesi

Corsica itself is wellness for all of the senses—an island with a warm breeze that touches the skin like silk, where the light is incomparably clear, and where a hint of pine and salt always lies in the air. Corsica combined with the Casadelmar is like a dream come true: Located on the southeast coast in the bay of Porto Vecchio, this little hotel links the poetry of nature with the design of the modern age. Built on the hillside, all 31 rooms and suites reveal cinematic panoramas of the ocean and mountains. They speak a simple, beautiful language of forms and set strong color accents with azure, strawberry red, chocolate brown, or violet that are a pleasure to the eye. The cuisine of chef Davide Bisetto, who has earned his stars, presents itself in the same genuine, surprising manner—with Italian-French creativity, he focuses on the fresh, aromatic ingredients of the island and conjures up filigree works of art on the plates. The relaxation at the Casadelmar spa is stylish and sophisticated (the skin-care products are by Carita and Decléor). The favorite spot of all the guests is the infinity pool—when it is illuminated at the blue hour and then glows like jade.

Korsika an sich ist schon Wellness für alle Sinne – eine Insel, deren warme Brise die Haut wie Seide berührt, wo das Licht unvergleichlich klar ist und wo immer ein Hauch von Pinien und Salz in der Luft schwebt. Korsika kombiniert mit dem Casadelmar ist wie ein Traum, der Wirklichkeit wurde: An der Südostküste in der Bucht von Porto Vecchio gelegen, verbindet dieses kleine Hotel die Poesie der Natur mit dem Design der Moderne. An den Hang gebaut, eröffnen alle 31 Zimmer und Suiten kinotaugliche Panoramen über Meer und Berge, sprechen eine schlicht-schöne Formensprache und setzen mit Azurblau, Erdbeerrot, Schokoladenbraun oder Violett kräftige Farbakzente, die einfach Spaß machen. So unverfälscht und überraschend präsentiert sich auch die Küche des sternegekrönten Chefs Davide Bisetto – er setzt mit italienisch-französischer Kreativität auf frische, aromatische Zutaten der Insel und zaubert filigrane Kunstwerke auf die Teller. Im Spa des Casadelmar entspannt man stilvoll und sophisticated (die Pflegeprodukte stammen von Carita und Decléor), und Lieblingsplatz aller Gäste ist der Infinity-Pool – wenn er zur blauen Stunde illuminiert wird und dann wie Jade leuchtet.

01 | Welcome: The entrance area with its Asian look.

Willkommen: Der asiatisch anmutende Eingangsbereich.

02
03
04

05

02 | Between the sky and the sea: The 82-foot infinity pool.
Zwischen Himmel und Meer: Der 25 Meter lange Infinity-Pool.

03 | Spots of color: Sun loungers on the beach of Porto Vecchio.
Farbtupfer: Sonnenliegen am Strand von Porto Vecchio.

04 | Classic in bright red: The wire armchair Bertoia by Knoll.
Klassiker in Knallrot: Der Drahtsessel Bertoia von Knoll.

05 | The lounge bar: Room to chat, read, and enjoy.
Die Lounge Bar: Platz zum Plaudern, Lesen, Genießen.

hôtel des lacs d'halco | hagetmau . france

DESIGN: Eric Raffy

This interesting hotel architecture by the Frenchman Eric Raffy can be found in the heart of Gascogne. His goal was to design a building that blends harmoniously into the surrounds. As a result, the two-story hotel building follows the course of the lake's shoreline in an arc. The facade facing the lake has glass from floor to ceiling so that people on the inside feel as if they were part of the landscape. The reflection of the hotel in the water creates the appearance of it merging completely with its environment. The rooms were furnished with the intention of extending the reflecting surface of the lake. This was done through room dividers of sandblasted mirror surfaces that serve as the bathroom mirror on one side and the bed's headboard on the other. Yet the connection with nature goes even further: In the combination of materials used for the structure—wood, stone, copper, and glass—an emphasis was placed on incorporating elements from the immediate surroundings. A floating rotunda is directly in front of the hotel and connected with it through a footbridge. This is where the restaurant is located. In this grand setting, chef Annie Demen offers deliciously prepared regional dishes with the complementary wines.

Im Herzen der Gascogne trifft man auf diese interessante Hotelarchitektur des Franzosen Eric Raffy. Sein Ziel war, ein Gebäude zu entwerfen, das sich harmonisch in die Umgebung einfügt. So folgt das zweigeschossige Hotelgebäude in einem Bogen dem Verlauf der Uferlinie des Sees. Die dem See zugewandte Fassade ist bis zum Boden verglast, so dass man im Inneren das Gefühl hat, Teil der Landschaft zu sein. Durch die Spiegelung des Hauses im Wasser scheint dieses förmlich mit seiner Umgebung zu verschmelzen. Bei der Zimmerausstattung wurde versucht, die spiegelnde Oberfläche des Sees fortzusetzen. Dies geschah in Form von Raumteilern aus sandgestrahlten Spiegelflächen, die von einer Seite als Badezimmerspiegel, von der anderen als Kopfteil des Bettes dienen. Aber die Verbindung mit der Natur geht noch weiter: Bei der Kombination der für den Bau verwendeten Materialien – Holz, Stein, Kupfer und Glas – wurde darauf geachtet, Elemente der nächsten Umgebung aufzunehmen. Dem Hotel vorgelagert ist eine schwimmende Rotunde, die mit dem Hotel über einen Steg verbunden ist. Hier befindet sich das Restaurant. In dieser grandiosen Kulisse bietet Küchenchefin Annie Demen köstlich zubereitete regionale Gerichte mit den dazu passenden Weinen an.

01 | The two-story hotel building follows the course of the lake's shoreline in an arc.

Das zweigeschossige Hotelgebäude folgt in einem Bogen dem Verlauf der Uferlinie.

02 03

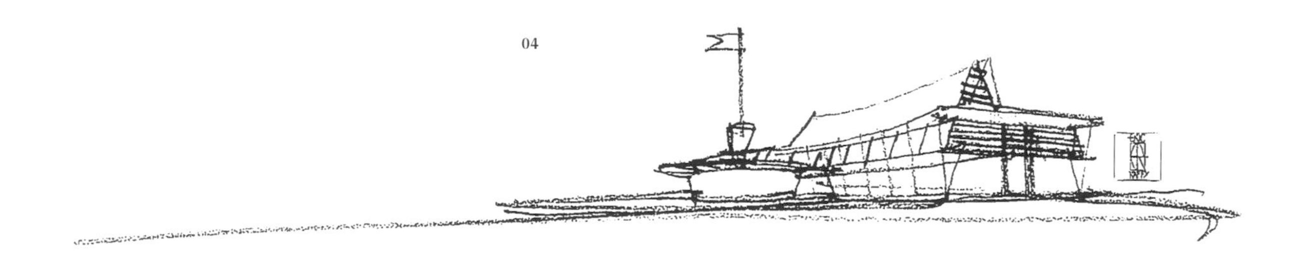

04

02 | Warm colors characterize the reception area.

Warme Farben prägen den Rezeptionsbereich.

03 | The three-star hotel offers 24 rooms with a view of the forest or lake.

Das Drei-Sterne-Haus bietet 24 Zimmer mit Wald- oder Seeblick.

04 | Scetch.

Skizze.

05 | The indoor pool invites guests for long swims on cold days.

An kalten Tagen lädt das Hallenbad zu ausgiebigem Schwimmen ein.

06 | The central point of the complex is the "island restaurant" in front of it.

Zentraler Punkt des Komplexes ist das vorgelagerte „Insel-restaurant".

07 | Plan.

Grundriss.

07

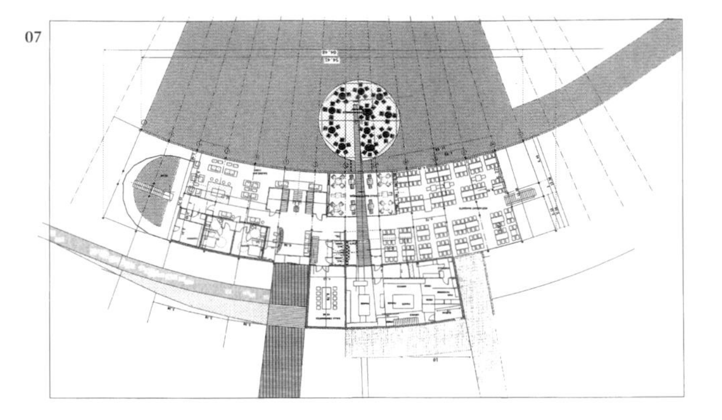

cowley manor | cowley . united kingdom

DESIGN: De Matos Storey Ryan

The Cowley Manor is situated grandly in rich green scenery, surrounded by wide forests and smaller lakes. The country residence is distinguished by a remarkable mixture of historic ambience and contemporary design. Despite the old origin of the house, the 30 guest rooms have been designed with a modern and individual approach. Light-colored wood in a clear vocabulary of form plays a central role here, just like the warm tones of the armchairs, curtains, and paintings on the wall. Curved furniture additionally brightens up the ensemble and illustrates the skillful integration of the modern at a site with walls so rich in history. But times past also have their place at Cowley Manor: The dark and artfully decorated wood of the paneling and ceilings in the hallways, staircase, and restaurant impart an impression of the hotel's previous splendor. On the other hand, the spa is modern and has already won a number of awards for its wellness program, as well as for its simple and transparent design. Two bright fenestrated facades are rhythmically organized just through thin ribs; supporting pillars and walls of granite hold the roof. The spa is a delight not just for the body and spirit, but also for the eyes.

Herrschaftlich liegt das Cowley Manor in einer satt grünen Landschaft, umgeben von weiten Wäldern und kleineren Seen. Der Landsitz zeichnet sich durch eine bemerkenswerte Mischung aus historischem Ambiente und zeitgemäßem Design aus, denn ungeachtet der alten Herkunft des Hauses wurden die 30 Gästezimmer modern und individuell gestaltet. Helles Holz in klarer Formensprache spielt dabei eine tragende Rolle, genau so wie die warmen Farbtöne der Sessel, Vorhänge und Gemälde an der Wand. Geschwungene Möbel lockern das Ensemble zusätzlich auf und veranschaulichen die gekonnte Integration der Moderne an einen Ort, dessen Mauerwerk so reich an Geschichte ist. Aber auch die vergangenen Zeiten haben ihren Platz im Cowley Manor: In den Gängen, dem Treppenhaus und im Restaurant vermitteln die dunklen und kunstvoll verzierten Hölzer der Wandverkleidungen und Decken einen Eindruck von der früheren Pracht des Hauses. Modern ist dagegen wieder das Spa, das sowohl für seine Wellness-Angebote wie für sein schlichtes und transparentes Design schon mehrere Preise gewonnen hat. Zwei lichte Fensterfronten werden nur durch dünne Rippen rhytmisch gegliedert; Stützpfeiler und Wände aus Granit tragen das Dach. Nicht nur für Körper und Geist, auch für die Augen ist das Spa eine Wonne.

01 | The award-winning design of the spa is fascinating because of its light and transparent architecture.

Das mehrfach ausgezeichnete Design des Spa besticht durch seine leichte und transparente Architektur.

02 | The reception area is also characterized by colorful, curved furniture.

Auch den Empfang prägen farbenfrohe, geschwungene Möbel.

03 | Spaciousness was more important in the design of the rooms than an optimal use of each area.

Geräumigkeit war für die Gestaltung der Zimmer wichtiger als eine optimale Raumnutzung.

04 | The dark and ornamented wood of the paneling in the restaurant reveals an impression of earlier times.

Im Restaurant vermitteln die dunklen und verzierten Hölzer der Wandverkleidungen einen Eindruck von früheren Zeiten.

the grove | chandler's cross . united kingdom

DESIGN: Fox Linton, Fitzroy Robinson

The Grove is sometimes also called "the country estate of London." When you stand in the middle of the 300-acre property in Hertfordshire, it is hardly conceivable that England's capital is just 40 minutes away. Once the manor house for the Earl of Clarendon, The Grove is now a luxury hotel with its own golf course that even experts like Gary Player praise to the skies. The interior design also attracts attention since it combines suggestions of classic country style with contemporary chic, luxurious opulence, and wonderfully offbeat extravagance—the British humor is simply undeniable. The modern rooms are housed in the West Wing while the main house (the mansion) offers the more decadent rooms in three variations: elegant with dark wood and crème tones, cool and inspired by Japanese nuances, or seductively sexy with eggplant-colored silk and velvet. The holistic Sequoia Spa, which pampers guests with Ayurvedic ESPA products and has an enchanting bamboo garden, also promises a feast for the senses. And no less than three restaurants prove that the fairytale of bad English food is now really outdated—the stylish Colette's with à la carte cuisine is highly recommended.

Der „Landsitz Londons" wird The Grove auch genannt – wenn man inmitten des 121 Hektar großen Grundstücks in Hertfordshire steht, ist es kaum vorstellbar, dass Englands Hauptstadt nur 40 Minuten entfernt liegt. Einst das Herrenhaus der Earls of Clarendon, ist The Grove heute ein Luxushotel mit eigenem Golfplatz, den selbst Experten wie Gary Player in höchsten Tönen loben. Auch das Interieurdesign macht von sich reden, kombiniert es doch Anklänge an den klassischen Countrystil mit zeitgemäßem Chic, luxuriöser Opulenz und herrlich schräger Extravaganz – der britische Humor lässt sich eben nicht verleugnen. Im Westflügel sind moderne Zimmer untergebracht, das Haupthaus („Mansion") beherbergt die dekadenteren Räume in drei Varianten: Elegant mit dunklem Holz und Cremetönen, kühl und von japanischen Nuancen inspiriert oder verführerisch sexy mit auberginefarbener Seide und Samt. Ein Fest für die Sinne verspricht auch das ganzheitliche Sequoia Spa, das mit ayurvedischen ESPA-Produkten verwöhnt und einen zauberhaften Bambusgarten besitzt. Und gleich drei Restaurants beweisen, dass die Mär vom schlechten englischen Essen nun wirklich Vergangenheit ist – besonders empfehlenswert ist das stylische „Colette's" mit À la carte-cuisine.

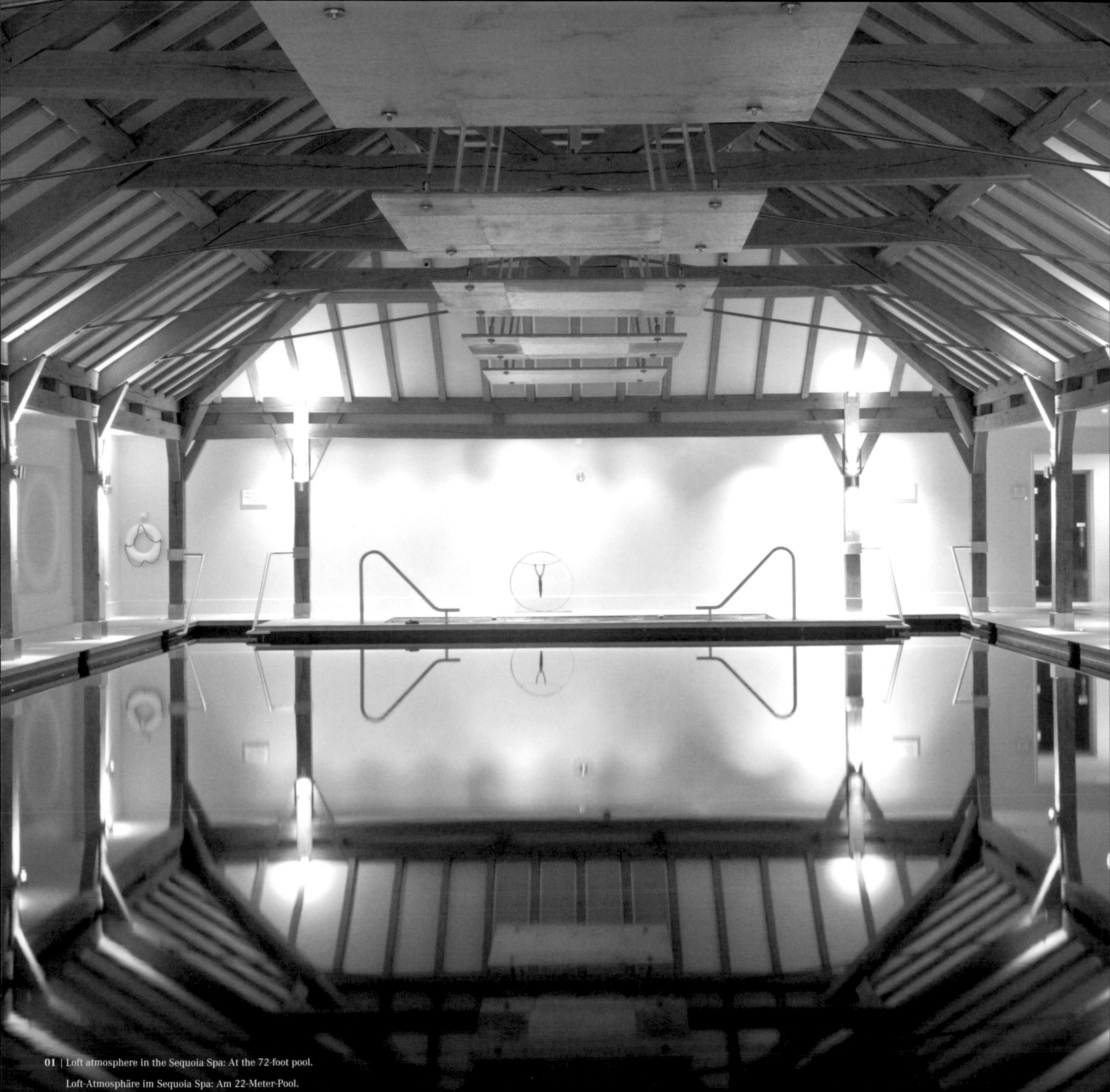

01 | Loft atmosphere in the Sequoia Spa: At the 72-foot pool.

Loft-Atmosphäre im Sequoia Spa: Am 22-Meter-Pool.

02 | Completely in keeping with British tradition: The conservatory.
Ganz nach britischer Tradition: Der Wintergarten.

03 | Far Eastern simplicity: The inner courtyard of the spa.
Von fernöstlicher Schlichtheit: Im Innenhof des Spas.

04 | A hint of the Orient: The Grove plays with styles.

Ein Hauch von Orient: The Grove spielt mit den Stilen.

05 | Country style with understatement: Favorite spots by the fireplace.

Countrystil mit Understatement: Lieblingsplätze am Kamin.

klaus k | helsinki . finland

DESIGN: SARC Architects (Antti-Matti Siikala, Sarlotta Narjos), Stylt Trampoli (Kajsa Krause)

Passion, mysticism, and desire: Inspired by the Finnish world of sagas, the room categories and the interior of the Hotel Klaus K symbolize the emotions of the creatures in the national epic Kalevala. Behind the room name of "Envy" are the largest suites in noble tones of gold and brown. The tragic antihero of the folk epic Klaus Kurki gave the hotel in the turn-of-the-century building its name. The concept comes from head designer Kajsa Krause. She sends guests on discovery journeys through the local cultures, an idea that also appeals to regular guests like Formula-1 star Mika Häkkinen. In each of the 137 rooms and suites, custom-made beds and mattresses provide extra comfort. The reading room with its pinecone brown Chesterfield sofas and heavy armchairs is reminiscent of an English university library. If you just want to be pampered, the hotel's own Helsinki Day Spa and Gym offers massages and fitness training. At this oasis in the middle of Helsinki's designer quarter, special value is placed on relaxation and harmony. High arched windows allow the mild light of the north to shine into the stucco-ornamented halls where upholstered loungers invited the guests to relax. And when it never gets quite dark during the summer solstice, the night owls meet in the hotel lounge called Ahjo—a name from Finnish mythology that promises good fortune and wealth.

Leidenschaft, Mystik, Verlangen: Inspiriert von der finnischen Sagenwelt symbolisieren die Zimmerkategorien und das Interieur im Hotel Klaus K die Emotionen der Wesen im Nationalepos „Kalevala". Hinter der Zimmerbezeichnung „Neid" verbergen sich die größten Suiten in edlen Gold- und Brauntönen. Der tragische Antiheld der Volksdichtung „Klaus Kurki" gab dem Hotel in dem Jahrhundertwendebau seinen Namen. Das Konzept stammt von Chefdesignerin Kajsa Krause. Sie schickt Gäste auf eine Entdeckungsreise der lokalen Kulturen, eine Idee, die auch Stammgästen wie dem Formel-1-Star Mika Häkkinen gefällt. In jedem der 137 Räume und Suiten sorgen maßgefertigte Betten und Matratzen für extra Komfort. Der Lesesaal erinnert mit tannenzapfenbraunen Chesterfieldsofas und schweren Sesseln an englische Universitätsbibliotheken. Wer sich einfach nur verwöhnen lassen möchte, dem bietet das hoteleigene „Helsinki Day Spa und Gym" Massagen- und Fitnesstraining. In der Oase mitten in Helsinkis Designerviertel wird besonderer Wert auf Entspannung und Harmonie gelegt. Hohe Bogenfenster lassen das milde Licht des Nordens in stuckverzierte Säle scheinen, wo gepolsterte Liegen zum Entspannen einladen. Und wenn es nachts zur Zeit der Sommersonnenwende nie ganz dunkel wird, trifft man Nachtschwärmer in der Hotellounge „Ahjo" – ein Name aus der finnischen Mythologie, der Glück und Reichtum verheißt.

01 | Guests can put together a tailor-made wellness program in the spa and sauna.

Im Spa und in der Sauna können sich Gäste ein maßgeschneidertes Wellnessprogramm zusammenstellen.

02 | Loungers invite guest to relax in the light-filled, sumptuously decorated large hall of the villa from the turn of the century.

Im lichten Prunksaal der Jahrhundertwendevilla laden Liegen zum Relaxen ein.

03 | Red velvet and indirect light characterize the suites with the theme of "Passion."

Roter Samt und indirektes Licht charakterisieren die Suiten mit dem Thema „Leidenschaft".

04 | Whether the daily newspaper or a novel: The library becomes a favorite spot with its Chesterfield sofa, chaise longue, and leather armchair.

Ob Tageszeitung oder Roman: Mit Chesterfield Sofa, Chaise Longue und Ledersessel wird die Bibliothek zum Lieblingsplatz.

hotel de rome | berlin . germany

DESIGN: Tommaso Ziffer, Olga Polizzi

With some luck, it is possible to meet Sir Rocco Forte in person at the Spa de Rome of his new luxury establishment on Berlin's Bebelplatz: The hotel owner is an enthusiastic athlete and had the pool extended by 65 feet beyond the original plan to he could swim longer laps. Jewels were once stored safely where the pool with its gold-colored Bisazza mosaic wall now waits for him and other swimmers—the Dresdner Bank had its headquarters in this magnificent building until 1945 and the vault was in this section. The long, eventful history of the hotel is an important component of its modern design, for which Sir Rocco's sister Olga Polizzi and Tommaso Ziffer are responsible. They let themselves be inspired in the design of the elegant rooms by Karl-Friedrich Schinkel and his neo-Classicist style, maintaining the stucco ceilings of up to 13 feet and classic proportions in many of the suites. The low points of history were also consciously not omitted: For example, there are still grenade splinters from the Second World War in some of the wood paneling. The Hotel de Rome is a successful example of how the past, present, and future can be combined in Berlin—and is definitely worth a visit.

Mit etwas Glück kann man Sir Rocco Forte höchstpersönlich im „Spa de Rome“ seiner neuen Luxusadresse am Berliner Bebelplatz treffen: Der Hotelchef ist passionierter Sportler und ließ den ursprünglich kleiner geplanten Pool auf 20 Meter verlängern, um besser Bahnen ziehen zu können. Wo heute das von einer goldfarbenen Bisazza-Mosaikwand begrenzte Becken auf ihn und weitere Schwimmer wartet, wurden einst Juwelen verwahrt – bis 1945 hatte die Dresdner Bank ihren Hauptsitz in diesem prachtvollen Gebäude und hier unten ihren Tresorraum. Die lange und abwechslungsreiche Geschichte des Hauses ist ein wichtiger Bestandteil des modernen Designs, für das sich Sir Roccos Schwester Olga Polizzi und Tommaso Ziffer verantwortlich zeichnen. Sie ließen sich bei der Gestaltung der eleganten Zimmer von Karl-Friedrich Schinkel und seinem neoklassizistischen Stil inspirieren und erhielten in vielen Suiten die bis zu vier Meter hohen Stuckdecken und klassischen Proportionen. Auch Tiefpunkte der Historie wurden bewusst nicht ausgespart: So stecken in einigen Holzvertäfelungen noch immer Granatsplitter aus dem Zweiten Weltkrieg. Das Hotel de Rome ist ein gelungenes Beispiel dafür, wie sich in Berlin Vergangenheit, Gegenwart und Zukunft verbinden lassen – es ist mehr als einen Besuch wert.

01 | The spa includes the pool, saunas, and six beauty cubicles.

Zum Spa gehören der Pool, Saunen und sechs Beautykabinen.

02 | The 146 rooms are decorated in the modern Berlin Style.

Die 146 Zimmer sind im modernen „Berlin Style“ gehalten.

03 | The Palm Court Ballroom is also used for meetings.

Der Palm Court-Ballsaal wird auch für Meetings genutzt.

04 | The Bebel Bar is located next to the Mediterranean Restaurant.

Die Bebel-Bar liegt neben dem mediterranen Restaurant.

q! | berlin . germany

DESIGN: Graft Architects

If you think that the hippest, trendiest, and hottest hotels of the German capital are just in Berlin-Mitte (center), you are wrong—and should let your eyes be opened in bourgeois Charlottenburg: Between the Ku'damm and Savignyplatz, Wolfgang Loock and Eva-Miriam Gerstner have opened the design hotel Q! and capitulated it into all of the hot lists of the international architecture, lifestyle, and travel magazines without wasting any time. You will look in vain for classic hotel design, right angles, and customary spatial concepts here—Q! relies on organic, flowing forms, and shows with its avangardistic style how hot cool design can be how hot cool design can be. You may sometimes feel like you are on board the Enterprise and then again on a James Bond set of the 1970s—and, in any case, it feels like the third millennium. The spa, with a relaxation room covered in the finest sand, is a small sensation in Berlin. The same applies to the bar, which is only open to hotel guests and club members. Q! was designed by the Graft architectural office, which also has Brad Pitt and Angelina Jolie among its clients. When the Hollywood couple came to Berlin, it reserved a night in Q!—and even left their hotel ... in Berlin-Mitte...for it.

Wer bislang dachte, dass die hippsten, trendigsten und angesagtesten Hotels der deutschen Hauptstadt ausschließlich in Berlin-Mitte stehen, irrt – und sollte sich im bourgeoisen Charlottenburg eines Besseren belehren lassen: Zwischen Ku'damm und Savignyplatz haben Wolfgang Loock und Eva-Miriam Gerstner das Designhotel Q! eröffnet und es ohne viel Umschweife auf sämtliche Hot Lists internationaler Architektur-, Lifestyle- und Reisemagazine katapultiert. Klassisches Hoteldesign, rechte Winkel und herkömmliche Raumkonzepte sucht man hier vergebens – das Q! setzt auf organische und fließende Formen und zeigt mit seinem avangardistischen Stil wie heiß cooles Design sein kann. Man fühlt sich bisweilen wie an Bord der Enterprise, dann wieder wie in einer James Bond-Kulisse der 1970er – und auf alle Fälle wie im dritten Jahrtausend. Das Spa, dessen Ruheraum feinster Sand bedeckt, ist in Berlin eine kleine Sensation; ebenso wie die Bar, die nur Hotelgästen und Clubmitgliedern offen steht. Entworfen wurde das Q! vom Architekturbüro Graft, das auch Brad Pitt und Angelina Jolie zu seinen Kunden zählt. Als das Hollywood-Paar nach Berlin kam, reservierte es eine Nacht im Q! – und verließ dafür sogar sein Hotel in... Berlin-Mitte.

01 | Relax: After the sauna, you can relax on the warm sand.

Entspannung: Nach der Sauna entspannt man auf warmem Sand.

02 | Eat, drink, and talk: In the Fusion Restaurant and bar.

Essen, Trinken & Reden: Im Fusion-Restaurant und in der Bar.

03

04

03 | Live: The Q! has 72 rooms, four studios, and one penthouse.

Erleben: Das Q! besitzt 72 Zimmer, vier Studios und ein Penthouse.

04 | Feel: High-quality materials are extras for all of the senses.

Fühlen: Hochwertige Materialien sind Extras für alle Sinne.

05 | Section.

Querschnitt.

05

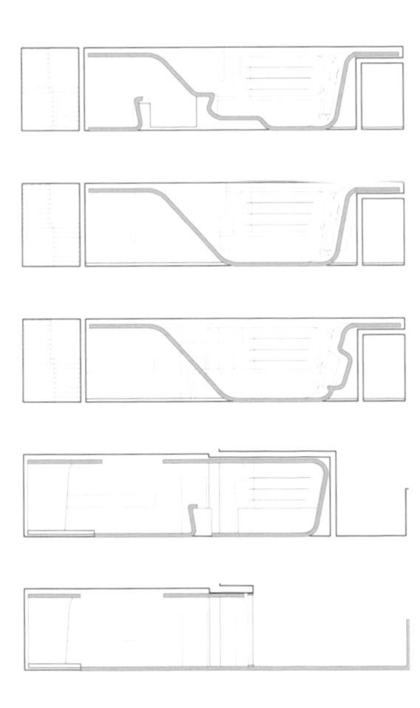

der oeschberghof | donaueschingen . germany

DESIGN: Markus-Diedenhofen

Take it easy for a few days. Let your soul unwind and clear your mind. Play a round of golf and dive into the pool: You don't always have to travel through half of Europe to find this—good things are sometimes closer than we think. Located just an hour south of Stuttgart, between the Black Forest and the Swabian Alb, the Öschberghof is a wonderful sanctuary for anyone who would like to combine design, wellness, and sport. Clear lines and high-quality materials, warm shades of brown, and artfully placed sources of light let the guest take a deep breath from the very first moment in the general areas and the 73 rooms. And the 5,900 square feet wellness world can hardly be surpassed in terms of variety. Ayurvedic affusions, packs in the hanging lounger, aroma massages, magnetic-field therapies, sauna sessions, pilates, or yoga: The wellness experts of the hotel fulfill almost every wish and increase the distance to everyday life by the minute. Golfers should add the appropriate start times to their personal-care program—after all, an 18-hole and a 9-hold course are available right in front of the door. And there's no need to worry that the rich Swabian food might ruin all of the wellness efforts—international and light meals are cooked at the Öschberghof.

Ein paar Tage ausspannen. Die Seele baumeln lassen und den Kopf frei bekommen. Eine Runde Golf spielen und im Pool abtauchen: Dafür muss man nicht immer durch halb Europa reisen – das Gute liegt manchmal näher als man denkt. Gerade einmal eine Stunde südlich von Stuttgart, zwischen Schwarzwald und Schwäbischer Alb, ist der Öschberghof ein wunderbares Refugium für alle, die Design, Wellness und Sport verbinden möchten. Klare Linien und edle Materialien, warme Brauntöne und raffiniert eingesetzte Lichtquellen lassen den Gast in den öffentlichen Bereichen und 73 Zimmern vom ersten Moment an aufatmen – und die 1800 Quadratmeter große Wellness-Welt ist an Vielfalt kaum zu übertreffen. Ayurveda-Güsse, Packungen in der Schwebeliege, Aromamassagen, Magnetfeldtherapien, Saunagänge, Pilates oder Yoga: Die Wohlfühl-Experten des Hotels erfüllen so gut wie jeden Wunsch und vergrößern den Abstand zum Alltag mit jeder Minute mehr. Golfer sollten ihr Pflegeprogramm um passende Startzeiten ergänzen – schließlich stehen direkt vor der Tür ein 18- und ein 9-Loch-Platz zur Verfügung. Und keine Sorge, dass üppige schwäbische Kost alle Wellnessbemühungen zunichte machen könnte – im Öschberghof wird international und leicht gekocht.

01 | Perfect match: Calm and clear design dominates at the hotel.

Perfektes Zusammenspiel: Im Hotel dominiert ruhiges und klares Design.

02

02 | Effective: The design of the lighting underscores the ambience.
Wirkungsvoll: Das Lichtdesign unterstreicht das Ambiente.

03 | Asian: Massages from the Far East can also be enjoyed at the spa.
Asiatisch: Im Spa genießt man auch Massagen aus Fernost.

04 | In a prime location: Relaxing loungers by the swimming pool.
In bester Lage: Ruheliegen am Swimming Pool.

tschuggen grand hotel | arosa . switzerland

DESIGN: Carlo Rampazzi (Hotel), Mario Botta (Spa)

The Tschuggen Grand Hotel is a pinnacle of the Swiss hotel trade—not only in the most literal sense of the word (it stands proudly in the town of Arosa with its elevation of 5,900 feet): This is where the Swiss star architect Mario Botta played his home advantage and opened the Tschuggen Bergoase in December of 2006. The majority of the Alpine spa covering 16,400 square feet was built directly into the rock in terraces—only the geometric-looking sails of glass and steel on top signal that a wellness wonderworld is concealed here. Botta relies on materials in their natural state like granite, glass, and maple wood; he plays with light, shadow, and water, creating an atmosphere full of space, harmony, and refined luxury. Body and soul come into balance even just by "being there"—pools, saunas, and massages from Europe and Asia, as well as an excellent medical wellness program intensify this effect. The two spa suites, with jacuzzis directly beneath the two glass sails, are especially beautiful. The Bergoase is connected with the hotel through a glass bridge—the establishment has also spared no efforts in terms of design: Carlo Rampazzi has remodeled the rooms with much color and a touch of humor.

Das Tschuggen Grand Hotel ist ein Höhepunkt der eidgenössischen Hotellerie – nicht nur im wahrsten Wortsinn (es thront im 1800 Meter hoch gelegenen Arosa): Hier hat der Schweizer Star-Architekt Mario Botta seinen Heimvorteil voll ausgespielt und im Dezember 2006 die Tschuggen Bergoase eröffnet. Der Großteil des 5000 Quadratmeter umfassenden Alpen-Spas wurde terrassenförmig direkt in den Fels gebaut – an der Oberfläche signalisieren nur geometrisch wirkende Segel aus Glas und Stahl, dass sich hier eine Wellness-Wunderwelt verbirgt. Botta setzt auf naturbelassene Materialien wie Granit, Glas und Ahornholz, spielt mit Licht, Schatten und Wasser und schafft eine Atmosphäre voller Raum, Harmonie und dezentem Luxus. Schon beim bloßen „Dasein" kommen Körper und Seele ins Gleichgewicht – Pools, Saunen, Massagen aus Europa und Asien sowie ein ausgezeichnetes Medical Wellness-Angebot verstärken diesen Effekt. Besonders schön sind die zwei Spa Suiten, deren Jacuzzis direkt unter zwei Glassegeln liegen. Die Bergoase ist über eine gläserne Brücke mit dem Hotel verbunden – im Haus wurden in punkto Design ebenfalls keine Mühen gescheut: Carlo Rampazzi hat die Zimmer mit viel Farbe und einem Hauch Humor neu gestaltet.

01 | Glass sails of up to 42 feet in height let the light flow in.

Bis zu 13 Meter hohe Glassegel lassen Licht einfließen.

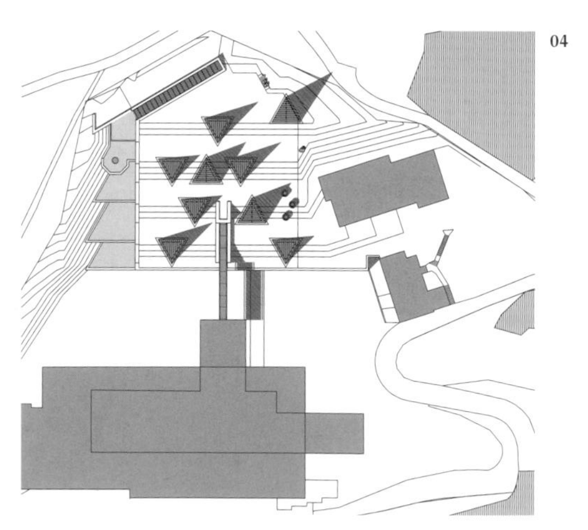

02 | The 130 rooms have panorama views.

Aus den 130 Zimmern eröffnen sich Panoramablicke.

03 | Carlo Rampazzi relies on color surfaces and a mix of patterns.

Carlo Rampazzi setzt auf Farbflächen und Mustermix.

04 | Top view.

Draufsicht.

05 | Tschuggen was created from a former sanitarium.

Das Tschuggen entstand aus einem ehemaligen Sanatorium.

06 | Rock, water, and light interact harmoniously with each other.

Fels, Wasser und Licht wirken harmonisch zusammen.

07 | The sails become illuminated works of art at night.

Nachts werden die Segel zu leuchtenden Kunstwerken.

05
06
07

la réserve genève hotel & spa | geneva . switzerland

DESIGN: Patrice Reynaud, Jacques Garcia

In the middle of a ten-acre park on the shore of Lake Geneva, where box trees have been pruned into peacocks and bears, lies a hidden jewel: the Hotel La Réserve Genève. The French interior designer Jacques Garcia transformed the building from the 1970s into a luxury resort with the help of rich colors, fine materials, and tropical timbers. The famous designer is a master at harmoniously connecting various styles with each other: Despite all the noblesse, the suites look comfortable and modern with gleaming parquet floors, black granite bathrooms, silk-taffeta curtains, and mahogany furniture. Striped lengths of material above the beds are reminiscent of tents inhabited by Oriental rulers, while the velvet-covered safari chairs, nostalgic travel photography, and framed tapestries conjure up the colonial age. And parrots of colorful resin bob on chandelier arms and lampshades. The resort's island of paradise is the spa with its fitness room, indoor and outdoor swimming pool, solarium, hair stylist, sauna, and hammam. The program offers: balneotherapy, scrubs, massages. The white health restaurant in art-déco style is illuminated diffusely by lamps in the shape of sea urchins. Incidentally: Anyone who would like to arrive unnoticed on the lake can simply be picked up by the elegant Venetian motoscafo or zoom from the hotel harbor for shopping in the city.

Inmitten eines vier Hektar großen Parks am Ufer des Genfer Sees, wo Buchsbäume zu Pfauen und Bären gestutzt sind, liegt ein verstecktes Juwel: das Hotel La Réserve Genève. Der französische Interieurdesigner Jacques Garcia verwandelte das Gebäude aus den 70er Jahren mit Hilfe satter Farben, edlen Stoffen und Tropenhölzern in ein Luxusresort. Der bekannte Gestalter ist ein Meister darin, unterschiedliche Stile harmonisch miteinander zu verbinden: Bei aller Noblesse wirken die Suiten behaglich und modern mit glänzenden Parkettböden, schwarzem Granitbädern, Seidentaft-Gardinen und Mahagonimöbeln. Gestreifte Stoffbahnen über den Betten erinnern an Zelte orientalischer Herrscher, mit Samt bespannte Safaristühle, nostalgische Reisefotografien und gerahmte Tapisserien an die Kolonialzeit. Und auf Leuchterarmen und Lampenschirmen wippen Papageien aus buntem Plexiglas. Trauminsel des Resorts ist der Spa mit Fitnesssaal, Hallen-und Freibad, Solarium, Coiffeursalon, Sauna und Hammam. Im Angebot: Blüten-Aromatherapie, Milchbäder und Schlankheitsmassagen. In dem schwarz-weißen, im Art déco-Stil gestylten Gesundheitsrestaurant verbreiten seeigelförmige Leuchten diffuses Licht. Übrigens: Wer unbemerkt über den See anreisen möchte, lässt sich einfach von dem eleganten venezianischen Motoscafo abholen oder düst vom Hotelhafen aus zum Shopping in die City.

01 | A mood of adventure like in an African lodge: The dining room with bamboo stakes and the replica of an elephant trophy in front of an iron-paneled fireplace.

Abenteuerstimmung wie in einer afrikanischen Lodge: Der Speisesaal mit Bambuspfählen und der Nachbildung einer Elefantentrophäe vor einem eisenvertäfelten Kamin.

02 | Crimson velvet armchair, rattan furniture, and a canopy of striped taffeta above the bed quote stylistic elements of the colonial age.

Purpurrote Samtsessel, Rattanmöbel und ein Himmel aus gestreiftem Taft über dem Bett zitieren Stilelemente der Kolonialzeit.

03 | A frieze of little golden mosaic stones lines the indoor swimming pool.

Ein Fries aus goldenen Mosaiksteinchen säumt das Hallenbad.

04 | The pool terrace offers lots of room for summer guests.

Jede Menge Platz für Sommergäste bietet die Poolterrasse.

05 | Art-déco chaise longue and jellyfish lamps in the Spa Séparée.

Art déco-Chaise Longue und Medusenleuchte im Spa-Séparée.

04 05

victoria-jungfrau grand hotel & spa | interlaken . switzerland

DESIGN: Wolfgang Behles, Ernst Anderegg, Jo Brinkmann

A picture-book landscape with glittering lakes and the raw Jungfrau Mountains is outside; but what is perhaps the most beautiful and stylish Grand Hotel of Switzerland awaits you on the inside: you will look in vain for thick carpets and dusty pomp and glamour in the Victoria-Jungfrau—instead, it offers 212 rooms and suites that are furnished in a chic, stylish, and sophisticated manner. Whether simple and elegant, luxurious and opulent, or spectacular like the white-yellow-black design of the Tower Suite in the tower's dome—all of the rooms have their individual face and demonstrate both good taste and a love of detail. This also applies to the Victoria-Jungfrau Spa with its impressive pool hall, which was designed as homage to the bathing culture of the Romans. A more purist approach can be seen in the Clarins Beauty Center and the ESPA area, where deeply relaxing oils and revitalizing sea products let stress and worries disappear (a hot tip for couples is the Private Spa Ritual—a pampering program à deux in a paradisiacal spa site). The wellness program is supplemented by a spa bar, at which the guests can enjoy light delicacies while in their bathrobes. If you feel more like dressing up in your fancy dining wardrobe, you can show it off in a place like La Terrasse—the French restaurant is among the best in Switzerland.

Draußen liegt eine Bilderbuchlandschaft mit glitzernden Seen und dem rauen Jungfraumassiv, drinnen wartet das vielleicht schönste und stilvollste Grand Hotel der Schweiz: Dicke Teppiche und verstaubten Glanz und Glamour sucht man im Victoria-Jungfrau vergebens – statt dessen findet man 212 Zimmer und Suiten, die schick, stilvoll und sophisticated ausgestattet sind. Ob schlicht-elegant, luxuriös-opulent oder spektakulär wie die weiß-gelb-schwarz designte Towersuite in der Turmkuppel – alle Räume haben ihr individuelles Gesicht und beweisen Geschmack sowie Liebe zum Detail. Das gilt auch für das Victoria-Jungfrau Spa mit seiner eindrucksvollen Poolhalle, die als Hommage an die Badekultur der Römer entworfen wurde. Puristischer geben sich das Clarins-Beautycenter sowie der ESPA-Bereich, wo tief entspannende Öle und revitalisierende Meeresprodukte Stress und Sorgen verschwinden lassen (ein Geheimtipp für Paare ist „The Private Spa Ritual“ – ein Verwöhnprogramm à deux in einer paradiesischen Spa-Suite). Ergänzt wird das Wellnessangebot durch eine Spa Bar, an der die Gäste im Bademantel leichte Köstlichkeiten genießen. Wem der Sinn eher nach großer Dinner-Garderobe steht, kann diese zum Beispiel im „La Terrasse“ zeigen – das französische Restaurant zählt zu den besten der Schweiz.

01 | Classically inspired: The 65-foot main pool.

Klassisch inspiriert: Der 20 Meter lange Hauptpool.

02 | Refined and elegant: the spa-suites.
Edel & elegant: Die Spa-Suiten.

03 | The power of the water: The whirlpool area in the spa.

Die Kraft des Wassers: Der Whirlpoolbereich im Spa.

04 | Artful: Modern design behind historic walls.

Geschickt: Modernes Design hinter historischen Mauern.

park hotel weggis | weggis . switzerland

DESIGN: Vincenz Erni, Aldoplan AG, Vadian Metting van Rijn, Pius Notter

This Jugendstil jewel lies at the center of a large park and has been made fit for the third millennium with great dedication. The entrepreneur Martin Denz, who already spent his vacations in Weggis as a child, created his very personal vision of a perfect vacation hotel here. The original beauty of the main house and the small castle was restored, while a contemporary, colorful design was realized in the interior. Fine materials like oiled American cherry or pale gray slate for the floors were combined with pieces of furniture and lamps by well-known designers such as Molteni, Cassina, and Philippe Starck. The Aquarius Hall for events in the Japanese Garden is avantgardist—a square, 20-foot high cube with a doubled shell of glass. In the facade of the hall, more than 90,000 little lamps ensure that it shines in a great variety of colors. New paths have also been taken in the wellness area with six individually equipped spa cottages that can be booked by the hour. The Asian-inspired architecture with natural, high-quality materials of stone and precious wood promises peace and quiet, as well as an exclusive experience of well-being.

Inmitten eines großen Parks liegt dieses Jugendstil-Kleinod, das mit viel Engagement fit gemacht wurde für das dritte Jahrtausend. Der Unternehmer Martin Denz, der schon als Kind seine Ferien in Weggis verbrachte, verwirklichte hier seine ganz persönliche Vision vom perfekten Ferienhotel. Die ursprüngliche Schönheit von Haupthaus und Schlössli wurde wieder hergestellt, im Inneren dagegen ein zeitgemäßes, farbenfrohes Design realisiert. Edle Materialien wie geölte amerikanische Kirsche oder mattgrauer Schiefer für die Böden wurden mit Möbeln und Leuchten bekannter Designer wie Molteni, Cassina und Philippe Starck kombiniert. Avantgardistisch ist die „Aquarius Hall" für Veranstaltungen im Japanischen Garten – ein rechteckiger, sechs Meter hoher Kubus mit einer doppelten Hülle aus Glas. In der Fassade der Halle sorgen 90 000 Lämpchen dafür, dass sie in den unterschiedlichsten Farben leuchtet.
Neue Wege beschritt man auch im Wellness-Bereich mit den sechs individuell ausgestatteten Spa-Cottages, die stundenweise gebucht werden können. Die asiatisch inspirierte Architektur mit natürlichen, hochwertigen Materialien aus Naturstein und Edelholz verspricht Ruhe und ein exklusives Wohlfühlerlebnis.

01 | A 72,000 square feet garden surrounds the Parkhotel Weggis.

Ein 22 000 Quadratmeter großer Garten umgibt das Parkhotel Weggis.

02

03

02 | The shore offers a wonderful panorama of the Central Swiss Alps.

Vom Ufer aus genießt man einen traumhaften Blick auf die Zentralschweizer Alpenkette.

03 | Section.

Schnitt.

04 | Six large spa cottages can be booked individually and offer wellness in a very private atmosphere.

Sechs große Spa-Cottages können einzeln gebucht werden und bieten Wellness in einer ganz privaten Atmosphäre.

05 | View from the Japanese Garden to the Aquarius Hall with its illumination in changing colors.

Blick vom Japanischen Garten auf die in wechselnden Farben beleuchtete „Aquarius Hall".

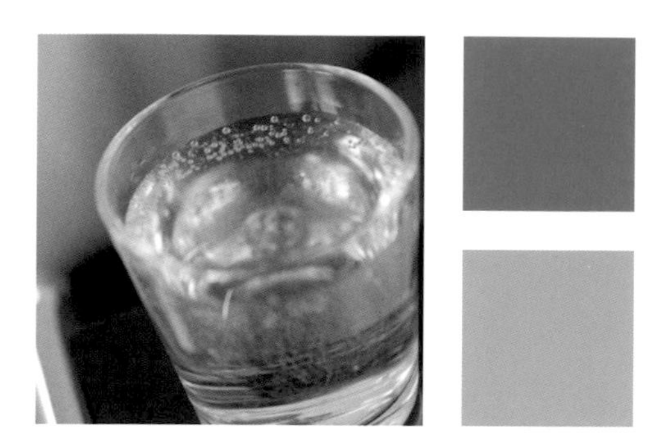

therme vals | vals . switzerland

DESIGN: Peter Zumthor

In earlier times, the little mountain village of Vals was primarily familiar to water gourmets for its mineral water. The thermal baths with their adjoining hotel now also attract people who are interested in architecture. Architect Peter Zumthor built the thermal baths from the stone of the surrounding area, which is called Valser quartzite. In precise layers, 60,000 stone plates have been piled into massive, supportive walls. The dark gray of the rock gives the structure an archaic look, yet the complex is never boring—even just through the various types of surface treatment from roughly hewn to polished stone, a great variability has been created. In addition, a virtuoso play of light and shadow develops during the course of the day. The individual pools are also different in their lighting and temperature: The program extends from an extremely cold ice bath to a flower bath and a steam bath. Various massages and aromatherapies serve the purpose of relaxation. Since Annalisa Zumthor and Pius Truffer took over management of the hotel building dating back to the 1960s, a fresh breeze is blowing there as well.

Früher war das kleine Bergdorf Vals vor allem bei Wassergourmets für sein Mineralwasser bekannt. Inzwischen ziehen die Therme mit angegliedertem Hotel aber auch an Architektur interessierte Menschen an. Der Architekt Peter Zumthor baute die Therme aus dem Gestein der Umgebung, dem Valser Quarzit. In präzisen Schichten sind 60 000 Steinplatten zu massiven, tragenden Wänden gestapelt worden. Das dunkle Grau des Felsgesteins verleiht dem Bau ein archaisches Gepräge, aber der Komplex wirkt trotzdem nie langweilig – denn allein durch die unterschiedlichen Arten der Oberflächenbearbeitung vom grob behauenen bis hin zum polierten Stein wurde eine sehr große Variabilität erzeugt. Außerdem entfaltet sich im Laufe eines Tages ein virtuoses Spiel aus Licht und Schatten. In Beleuchtung und Temperatur unterscheiden sich auch die einzelnen Wasserbecken: das Angebot reicht vom extrem kalten Eisbad übers Blütenbad bis hin zum Dampfbad. Zur Entspannung dienen verschiedene Massagen und Aromatherapien. Seit Annalisa Zumthor und Pius Truffer die Führung des Hotelbaus aus den sechziger Jahren übernahmen, weht auch dort ein frischer Wind.

01 | The interplay of material and light in the thermal baths is incomparable.
Unvergleichlich in den Thermen ist das Spiel mit Material und Licht.

02 | The water of the inner pool goes all the way to the wall.

Das Wasser im inneren Becken reicht bis an die Wände.

03 | The quiet zone allows an enjoyable view of the Alpine landscape.

Von der Ruhezone genießt man den Blick auf die Alpenlandschaft.

04 | White cement floors, colorful carpets, and specially designed furniture characterize the newly decorated rooms.

Weiße Zementböden, bunte Teppiche und eigens entworfene Möbel prägen die neu gestalteten Zimmer.

05 | Plan of site.

Lageplan.

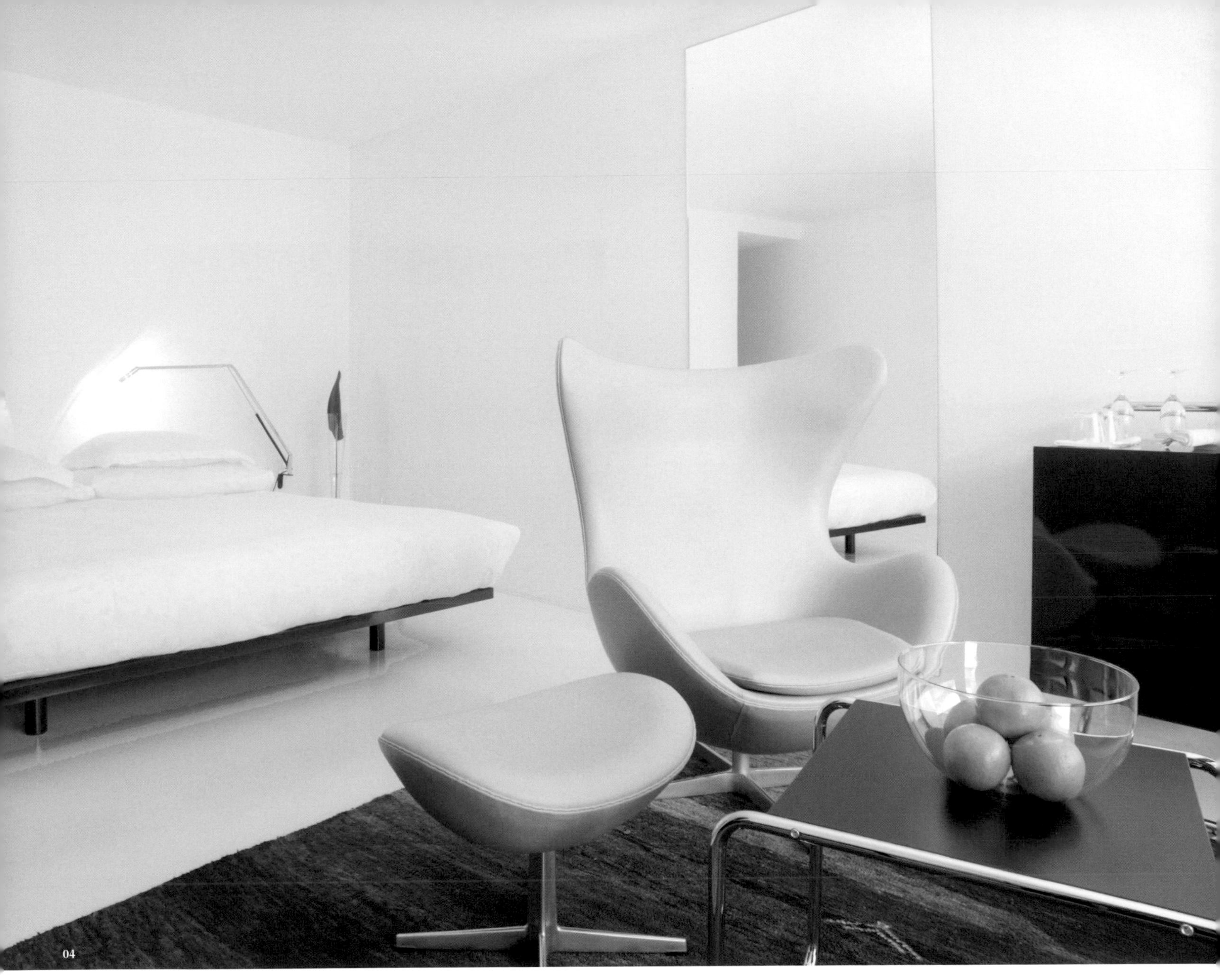
04

05
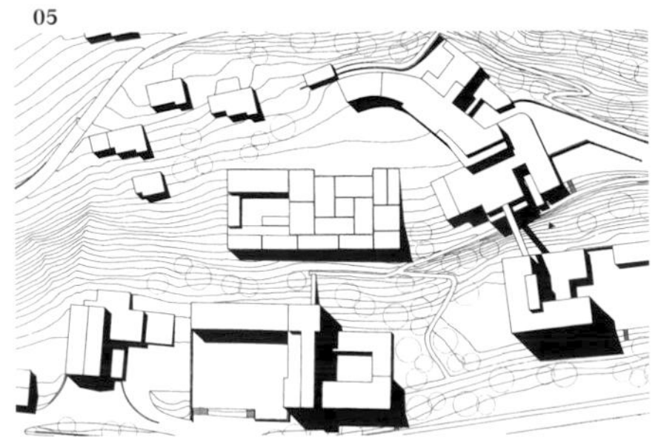

the omnia | zermatt . switzerland

DESIGN: Ali Tayar

Anyone who vacations here wants to be at the top. With the impressive backdrop of the majestic Matterhorn, the Mountain Lodge nestles into a steep slope above the posh Swiss ski resort of Zermatt. From here, an elevator concealed in the cliff transports hotel guests to the lobby at 5,410 feet. The modern mountain palace—which would also easily fit in a James Bond film – is surrounded by snow-covered woodland in winter. Gentian and clover blossom on the alpine pastures encircle it in the summer. Most of the balconies offer a breathtaking panorama of the 10,000 to 13,000 foot mountains Rothorn, Stockhorn, Gornergrat, Monte Rosa, and the Matterhorn. The panorama can also be enjoyed during a yoga class on the terrace, after a relaxing bath in the flower room, or during après ski in the outdoor whirlpool. The hotel of wood, glass, and steel was built by the New York architect Ali Tayar according to the American model. He let himself be inspired by American Modernism in the design of the 30 suites and the lounge areas. In addition to extravagantly manufactured fitted furniture of oak wood, he selected, in collaboration with Maryana Bilsky, pieces by designers such as Mies van der Rohe, Raymond Loewy, Vladimir Kagan, and Eero Saarinen—all of whom have strongly influenced this style with their European roots. He coordinated the shades of the upholstery and covers with the gray-green nuances of the rock formations and vegetation of the surroundings—and has created a sanctuary of the highest standards.

Wer hier Urlaub macht, will hoch hinaus. Vor der beeindruckenden Kulisse des majestätischen Matterhorns schmiegt sich die Mountain Lodge an einen Steilhang über dem noblen Schweizer Skiort Zermatt. Von dort aus transportiert ein im Felsen versteckter Lift Hotelgäste in die Lobby auf 1649 Metern Höhe. Im Winter umgeben dick verschneite Nadelwälder den modernen Bergpalast, der auch problemlos in einen James Bond Film passen würde. Im Sommer erblühen rund herum Enzian und Klee auf den Almwiesen. Von den meisten Balkonen aus bietet sich eine atemberaubende Rundsicht auf die Drei- und Viertausender Rothorn, Stockhorn, Gornergrat, Monte Rosa und Matterhorn. Auch bei einer Yogastunde auf der Terrasse, nach einem entspannten Bad im Blütenraum oder beim Aprés-Ski im Outdoor Whirlpool lässt sich das Panorama genießen. Das Hotel aus Holz, Glas und Stahl hat der New Yorker Architekt Ali Tayar nach amerikanischem Vorbild erbaut. Bei der Gestaltung der 30 Suiten und der Loungebereiche ließ er sich vom „Amerikanischen Modernismus" inspirieren. Neben aufwändig gefertigten Einbauten aus Eichenholz wählte er, in Zusammenarbeit mit Maryana Bilsky, Möbel von Designern wie Mies van der Rohe, Raymond Loewy, Vladimir Kagan und Eero Saarinen, die mit ihren europäischen Wurzeln diesen Stil stark geprägt haben. Die Farbtöne von Polstern und Bezügen stimmte er auf die grau-grünen Nuancen der Felsformationen und Vegetation der Umgebung ab – und zauberte ein Refugium auf höchstem Niveau.

01 | Burning torches line the pool, which extends out to the viewing terrace.

Brennende Fackeln säumen den Pool, der sich bis hinaus auf die Aussichtsterrasse erstreckt.

02 | If you are lucky, you will discover a buzzard on the hunt from the tower room.

Wer Glück hat entdeckt vom Turmzimmer aus einen Bussard auf der Jagd.

03 | The open fire in the rugged natural-stone walls exudes a chalet character.

Chaletcharakter verströmt das Kaminfeuer in der schroffen Natursteinmauer.

04 | The view from the southern balcony offers a view of the gabled roofs in car-free Zermatt.

Von dem Südbalkon aus blickt man auf die Giebeldächer im autofreien Zermatt.

hotel post | bezau . austria

DESIGN: Oskar Leo Kaufmann, Johannes Kaufmann

In a certain sense, the Bregenz Forest with its portly houses covered in wood shingles seems a bit sleepy. But this impression is misleading, at least in terms of building because the Austrian region of Vorarlberg is an Eldorado for anyone interested in contemporary architecture. One of its representatives is the young architect Oskar Leo Kaufmann. He designed an annex for his sister Susanne's hotel, which has already been run by the family for five generations. In just six weeks, this annex was built from a wooden-box system. The modules for it were completely prefabricated in the carpenter's workshop. The transparency of this architecture also allows much space for the surrounding world of nature, the soft alpine pastures of the Bödele and the rich meadows directly in front of the door. The rooms with their avantgardist furnishings are intended as a conscious contrast to the traditional original building. Some of its newly designed rooms convey a contemporary elegant atmosphere. The original tiles from the 1970s with their floral patterns were left in the bathrooms almost as a gimmick. The indoor swimming pool also comes from earlier decades, but has now been supplemented by a pretty outdoor pool, saunas, and a professional beauty area.

Auf eine gewisse Art ein wenig verschlafen wirkt der Bregenzerwald mit seinen behäbigen holzschindelverkleideten Häusern. Aber dieser Eindruck täuscht, zumindest, was das Bauen betrifft. Denn der österreichische Vorarlberg ist ein Eldorado für alle, die sich für zeitgenössische Architektur interessieren. Einer ihrer Vertreter ist der junge Architekt Oskar Leo Kaufmann. Er entwarf einen Anbau für das Hotel seiner Schwester Susanne, das die Familie bereits in fünfter Generation führt. In nur sechs Wochen wurde dieser Anbau im Holz-Box-System errichtet – die dafür verwendeten Module wurden in der Schreinerei komplett vorgefertigt. Die Transparenz dieser Architektur ließ auch viel Raum für die umliegende Natur, die sanften Almen des Bödele und die satten Wiesen direkt vor der Haustür. Die avantgardistisch eingerichteten Zimmer sollten einen bewussten Kontrast zum gutbürgerlichen Stammhaus bilden. Dort vermitteln einige neu gestaltete Zimmer eine zeitgemäß elegante Atmosphäre. Quasi als Gag wurden in den Bädern die original 70er Jahre Fliesen mit ihren typischen Blumenmustern erhalten. Auch das Hallenbad stammt aus früheren Jahrzehnten, inzwischen wurde es aber durch einen schmucken Außenpool, Saunen und einen professionellen Beautybereich ergänzt.

01 | Wood construction is also omnipresent in the indoor swimming pool.

Auch im Hallenbad sind Holzkonstruktionen allgegenwärtig.

02

02 | Transparency is attained through a successful combination of wood and glass.

Transparenz wird durch die gelungene Verbindung von Holz und Glas erreicht.

03 | Views.

Ansichten.

03

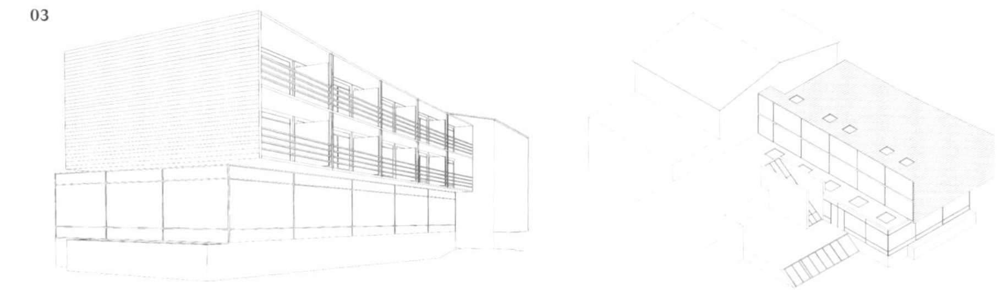

04

05

04 | The bathrooms are separated solely by a glass membrane from the sleeping area.

Die Bäder sind nur durch eine Glasmembran vom Schlafbereich getrennt.

05 | Floor plan.

Grundriss.

design hotel madlein | ischgl . austria

DESIGN: Sabine Mescherowsky, Gregor Mescherowsky

Hotelier Günther Aloys has created a site of contemplative peace and quiet in the winter resort of Ischgl - of all places - with its lively après-ski activities. He just considers this to be logical. "You have to make a peaceful spot precisely here in this hell," is his creed. The architecture of his hotel—which was inspired by the Far-Eastern philosophy of Zen—also plays with contrasts. It was designed by the Aachen-based architect couple Mescherowsky. The materials of stone, wood, and glass have been selected in such a way as to sensitize visitors to the opposites of hot and cold, rough and smooth. The large granite plates covering the floor of the spa area have been sandblasted, resulting in a velvety surface that delights the feet. Paths of teak plates connect the indoor swimming pool, the beauty area, and the saunas. In addition, the gigantic glass fronts allow the transition between the interior and the mountain world to become flowing and open the view of the purist Zen garden. The rooms are designed in a minimalist fashion that dispenses with anything that just has a decorative purpose. Mauve-stained wood harmonizes perfectly with the gray soft seating furniture and the whitewashed, matt oak parquet. Glass walls also serve as a transparent separation between the generous baths and the sleeping area here.

Ausgerechnet im Wintersportort Ischgl mit seinem lebendigen Après-Ski-Treiben hat der Hotelier Günther Aloys einen Ort kontemplativer Ruhe geschaffen. Für ihn selbst ist das nur konsequent. „Genau in diese Hölle musst du einen Ruhepunkt setzen", lautet sein Credo. Mit Kontrasten spielt auch die Architektur seines von der fernöstlichen Zen-Philosophie inspirierten Hotelanbaus, gestaltet vom Aachener Architektenpaar Mescherowsky. Die Materialien Stein, Holz und Glas sind so gewählt, dass sie für die Gegensätze heiß und kalt, rau und glatt sensibilisieren. Die großen Grantitplatten, mit denen der Spa-Bereich ausgelegt ist, wurden sandgestrahlt und bekamen auf diese Weise eine samtige Oberfläche, die den Füßen schmeichelt. Wege aus Teakholzplatten verbinden das Hallenbad, den Beauty-Bereich und die Saunen. Zudem lassen riesige Glasfronten den Übergang zwischen dem Inneren und der Bergwelt fließend werden und geben den Blick frei auf den puristischen Zengarten. Die Zimmer sind minimalistisch gestaltet, auf Nur-Dekoratives wurde verzichtet. Das mauvefarbig gebeizte Holz harmoniert perfekt mit den grauen weichen Sitzmöbeln und dem gekalkten, matten Eichenparkett. Glaswände dienen auch hier als transparente Trennung zwischen den großzügigen Bädern und dem Schlafbereich.

01 | Only a thin glass wall separates this spectacular room of water from the outside world.

Lediglich eine dünne Glaswand trennt diesen spektakulären Raum des Wassers von der Außenwelt.

02

02 | An Asiatic Zen garden in the middle of the Austrian Alps.

Ein asiatischer Zengarten mitten in den österreichischen Alpen.

03 | The fire room is a place of meditative quiet.

Ein Ort meditativer Ruhe ist der Feuerraum.

04 | The wellness center with a view of the indoor pool.

Wellnesszentrum mit Blick ins Hallenbad.

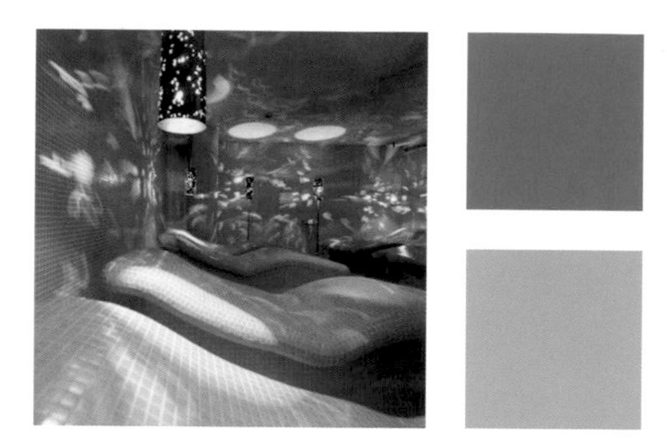

wine & spa resort loisium hotel | langenlois . austria

DESIGN: Steven Holl

Avantgardist world-class architecture and an ancient wine kingdom blend near the town of Langelois into a new type of unity. The wine & spa resort LOISIUM hotel close to Vienna at the gates of the Wachau region is the work of the American star architect Steven Holl—a futuristic, aluminum-faced vision that has no ambition of being a design hotel but one of the first architecture hotels. The facade with bands of light running through it rests on a glass base that gives the spectacular structure a sense of lightness. Beneath it are wine vaults dating back more than 900 years. Yet, the largest winegrowing area of the country—Grüner Veltliner is the best-known wine of the region—characterizes not only the surroundings but also a unique spa for fans of good wine. The first Aveda Destination Spa of Austria with a large observation deck and sun terrace is concealed behind the aluminum-faced facade. It offers Finnish, amethyst, and soft saunas, as well as aroma steam baths, a wine library in front of an open fireplace, fresh fruit, nuts, and tea at the spa bar, and hanging loungers in the garden. From here, guests can let their eyes wander across the surrounding vines after wine therapy with grape extracts.

Avantgardistische Weltklassearchitektur und uralte Weinwelt verschmelzen nahe der barocken Stadt Langenlois zu einer neuartigen Einheit. Das wine & spa resort LOISIUM Hotel nahe Wien vor den Toren der Wachau, ist das Werk des amerikanischen Stararchitekten Steven Holl – eine futuristische, aluminiumverkleidete Vision, die kein Designhotel, sondern eines der ersten Architekturhotels sein will. Die mit Lichtbändern durchzogene Fassade ruht auf einem gläsernen Sockel, der dem spektakulären Bau Leichtigkeit verleiht. Darunter liegen die über 900 Jahre alten Weingewölbe. Das größte Weinanbaugebiet des Landes – Grüner Veltliner ist der bekannteste Tropfen der Region – prägt jedoch nicht nur die Umgebung, sondern auch einen einzigartigen Spa für Freunde guten Weines. Hinter der aluminiumverkleideten Fassade versteckt sich der erste Aveda Destination Spa in Österreich mit großem Aussichtsdeck und Sonnenterrasse. Geboten werden finnische, Amethyst- und Soft- Sauna, Aroma Dampfbäder, eine Weinbibliothek vor einem offenen Kamin, frisches Obst, Nüsse, Tee an der Spa Bar und „Schwebeliegen“ im Garten. Von hier aus können Gäste nach einer Weintherapie mit Traubenextrakten den Blick über die umliegenden Rebstöcke schweifen lassen.

01 | The greatest possible contrast to the idyllic vineyards has been created by the American Steven Holl with his radical-modern hotel cube.

Den größtmöglichen Kontrast zu den idyllischen Weinbergen erzeugte der Amerikaner Steven Holl mit seinem radikal-modernen Hotelkubus.

02

04 05

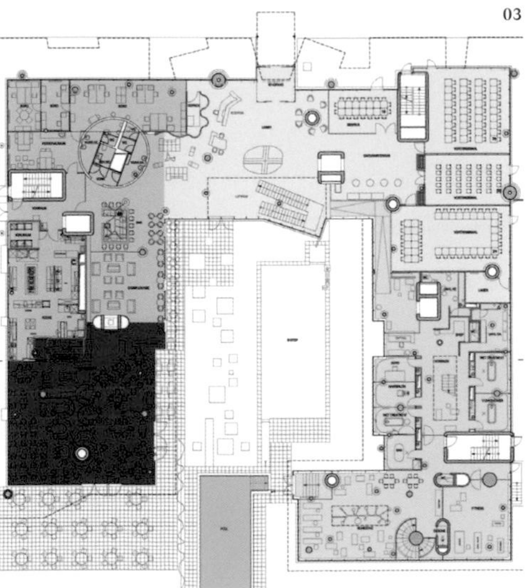
03

02 | The jade-green spa extends over two stories. The "upper deck" offers a panorama view across the vineyards.

Der jadegrüne Spa erstreckt sich über zwei Etagen. Das „Oberdeck“ bietet einen Panoramablick über die Weinberge.

03 | Floor plan.

Grundriss.

04 | Artful light effects, high atriums, and overlapping rooms are trademarks of the New York star architect Steven Holl.

Raffinierte Lichteffekte, hohe Atrien und ineinander übergreifende Räume sind Markenzeichen des New Yorker Stararchitekten Steven Holl.

05 | The decor on the mustard-colored upholstery symbolizes the paths and corridors in the ancient wine cellars beneath the hotel.

Das Dekor auf den senffarbenen Polstern symbolisiert die Wege und Gänge in den uralten Weinkellern unter dem Hotel.

mavida balance hotel & spa | zell am see . austria

DESIGN: Niki Szilagy

The focus is on the human being here. The design of the hotel keeps a genteel low profile. The Mavida Balance in the sport region of Kaprun on crystal-clear Lake Zell relies on deep relaxation, mental coaching, exercise, and—naturally—on pleasure. Together with the guest, the highly qualified team of the Fitness and Impulse Center strives for individualized treatments—from the beauty sessions and steam bath to the Kneipp treatments and body-forming to yoga, qi gong, and pilates. If you like, you can also revive your spirits with a bath in the ice fountain, drift away from everyday life in a unique floating pool, or enjoy the mountain panorama of the Alps while wrapped in a wool blanket on the balcony. The common rooms are also cozy relaxation zones through the light wood, tiles of matt slate, and natural-stone floors. The midnight blue and dark-red flower patterns on the textiles by the British designer Tricia Guild just catch your eye here and there. Reading islands in the library and a small open fireplace in each room promise leisurely hours. Valuable ingredients for the vitality meals in the restaurant are provided by the little herbal oasis on the fourth floor. The wine reserves are stored in a walk-in glass cube at the center of the restaurant. In the evening, people meet at the bar and in the lounge area for cool jazz sounds.

Hier steht der Mensch im Mittelpunkt. Die Gestaltung des Hotels nimmt sich vornehm zurück. Das Mavida Balance in der Sportregion Kaprun am glasklaren Zeller See setzt auf Tiefenentspannung, mentales Coaching, Bewegung und natürlich auf Genuss. Gemeinsam mit dem Gast sucht das hochqualifizierte Team des „Fitness und Impuls Centers“ nach individuell abgestimmten Anwendungen – von Beauty-Behandlungen und Dampfbad über Kneippkuren und Bodyforming bis hin zu Yoga, Qi Gong und Pilates. Wer möchte, weckt seine Lebensgeister auch mit einem Bad im Eisbrunnen, entschwebt dem Alltag in einem einzigartigen Floating-Becken oder genießt auf dem Balkon in eine Wolldecke gehüllt, das Bergpanorama der Alpen. Auch die Gemeinschaftsräume werden durch natürliche Materialien wie helles Holz, Fliesen aus mattem Schiefer und Natursteinböden zu wohnlichen Ruhezonen. Nur hier und da blitzen die mitternachtsblauen und dunkelroten Blumenmuster auf den Textilien der britischen Designerin Tricia Guild auf. Leseinseln in der Bibliothek und ein kleiner offener Kamin im eigenen Zimmer versprechen Mußestunden. Wertvolle Zutaten für die Vitalgerichte im Restaurant liefert die kleine Kräuteroase auf der dritten Etage. In dem begehbaren Glaskubus mitten in dem Lokal lagert der Weinvorrat. Und abends trifft man sich an der Bar und im Loungebereich zu coolen Jazzklängen.

01 | Rattan armchairs invite guests to unwind with a view of the snow-covered mountain peaks.

Rattansessel laden zum Erholen mit Blick auf die schneebedeckten Berggipfel ein.

02 | No conspicuous design distracts the attention in the spa with its minimalist décor.

In dem minimalistisch gestalteten Spa lenkt kein auffälliges Design die Aufmerksamkeit ab.

03 | Campfire romance with fine furnishings at the fireplace of the lounge bar.

Lagerfeuerromantik mit edler Ausstattung am Kamin der Loungebar.

04 | Sisal carpets, natural-stone plates, sand-colored walls, and a crackling fireplace—a cozy ambience for the soul.

Sisalteppiche, Natursteinplatten, sandfarbene Wände und ein prasselndes Kaminfeuer – wohnliches Ambiente für die Seele.

05 | Rooms with a wellness factor. Generous rooms in a clear, calm design invite you to stay for a while.

Zimmer mit Wellnessfaktor: Großzügige Räume in klarem ruhigen Design laden zum Verweilen.

vigilius mountain resort | lana . italy

DESIGN: Matteo Thun

There is no street leading to vigilius mountain resort. It does not have car noise or vehicles coming and going. You can only get to vigilius with the cabel railway. When you get off to enter the lobby of the hotel, you will be greeted by a simple architecture with a clear use of lines. The Milan architect Matteo Thun integrated the austerity of the buildings typical for this region—which fit well into the precipitous mountain world in material and form—into his design. The grass-covered roof of the vigilius is an esthetic and ecological memento of the surrounding nature. Fine larch wood and materials in natural tones create the framework for spaces of letting go and concentrating. Ceiling-high fenestrated facades impart an open, light-filled atmosphere. Anyone passing by the heated clay wall that seperates the bathing and living space will already suspect the delights that await body and soul in the spa of the house. A steam bath, an indoor and outdoor whirlpool, a swimming pool, and various treatments provide an all-round sense of well-being. The sauna, separated only from the amazing mountains by glass, are magnificent. Clear lines and a certain generosity also distinguish the 35 rooms and six suites. Natural materials and warm colors promote the pleasant peace and quiet and harmony.

Keine Straße führt zum vigilius mountain resort. Es gibt keinen Autolärm, kein An- und Abfahren. Ins vigilius geht es ausschließlich per Seilbahn. Wer von dort in die Lobby des Hotels tritt, wird von einer schlichten Architektur in klarer Linienführung empfangen. Der Mailänder Architekt Matteo Thun nahm in seinem Entwurf Bezug auf die Strenge der für die Region typischen Bauten, die sich in Material und Form gut in die schroffe Bergwelt einfügen. Das grasbedeckte Dach des vigilius ist eine ästhetische wie ökologische Reminiszenz an die umgebende Natur. Warmes Lärchenholz und Stoffe in Naturtönen schaffen den Rahmen für Räume des Loslassens und der Konzentration. Raumhohe Fensterfronten vermitteln eine offene, lichtdurchflutete Atmosphäre. Wer an dem beheizten Mauerwerk aus Stampflehm vorbeigeht, das Bad- und Wohnraum trennt, ahnt dabei schon die Wonnen, die im Spa des Hauses auf Körper und Seele warten. Ein Dampfbad, ein In- und Outdoor-Whirlpool, ein Schwimmbad und verschiedene Anwendungen sorgen für ein Rundum-Wohlbefinden. Großartig ist die Sauna, die nur durch Glas von den energiebeladenen Bergen getrennt sind. Die 35 Zimmer und sechs Suiten zeichnen sich ebenfalls durch klare Linien und eine gewisse Großzügigkeit aus. Natürliche Materialien und warme Farben begünstigen eine angenehme Ruhe und Harmonie.

01 | The glass fronts offer a marvelous view of the surrounding mountain world.

Durch die Glasfronten bietet sich eine herrliche Sicht auf die umliegende Bergwelt.

02 | 03 | The main concern of vigilius was integration into pristine nature in terms of the appearance and the use of wood and glass as materials.

Das Hauptanliegen des vigilius war die Integration in die unberührte Natur, sowohl im Erscheinungsbild wie auch bei den Materialien Holz und Glas.

04 | Heated clay walls seperate living and sleeping space from the baths.

Beheizte Wände aus Stampflehm trennen Wohn- und Schlafraum von den Bädern.

05 | Matteo Thun's first Mountain resort promises a new combination of architecture, mountain world, and wellness.

Matteo Thuns erstes Mountainresort verspricht eine neuartige Kombination aus Architektur, Bergwelt und Wellness.

06 | Sketch.

Skizze.

05

06
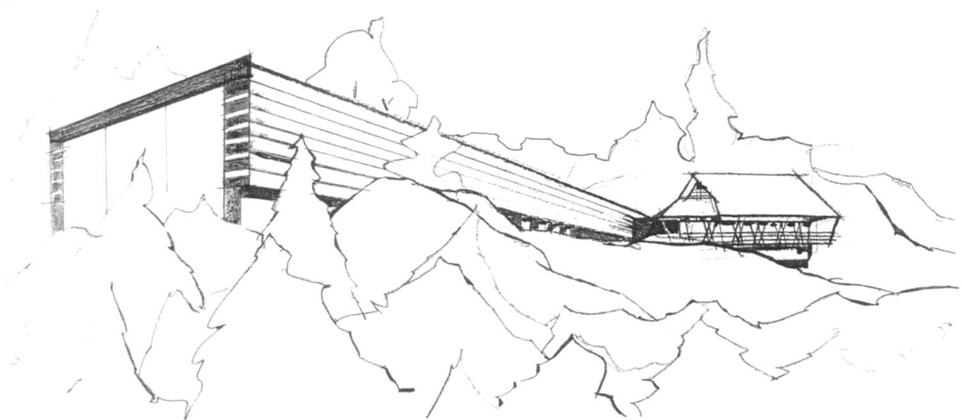

bulgari milan | milan . italy

DESIGN: Antonio Citterio and Partner

The name bears an obligation: This hotel in Milan's most elegant quarter is a genuine jewel. In the middle of a 13,000 square feet private garden that has been designed as a green oasis, the Bulgari combines history and the present. Parts of the building date back to the 18th century; the historic substance was intelligently combined with modern Italian design by Antonio Citterio & Partner. Valuable and rare materials like black marble from Zimbabwe, stone from Vicenza, and teak and oak give style and substance to the rooms and suites. Avant-garde details and state-of-the-art technology complete the "tribute to the world of luxury" that the Bulgari selected as its leitmotif in the design of the hotel. Every guest should be sure to visit the sensual spa with a gold-mosaic pool and green shimmering hammam—the beauty treatments and massages with fragrant essences symbolize la dolce vita in its loveliest form. The lounge and restaurant with its national cuisine have also dedicated themselves to the Italian approach to life. There is a direct view of the verdancy through high panorama windows during the meal—the gorgeous terrace is also open on warm days.

Der Name verpflichtet: Dieses Hotel in Mailands elegantestem Viertel ist ein echtes Schmuckstück. Inmitten eines 4000 Quadratmeter großen Privatgartens gelegen, der als grüne Oase gestaltet wurde, verbindet das Bulgari Historie und Gegenwart. Teile des Gebäudes datieren bis ins 18. Jahrhundert zurück; die historische Substanz wurde von Antonio Citterio & Partner intelligent mit modernem italienischem Design kombiniert. Wertvolle und seltene Materialien wie schwarzer Marmor aus Simbabwe, Stein aus Vicenza, Teak und Eiche geben den Zimmern und Suiten Stil und Substanz. Avantgardistische Details und aktuellste Technik vervollständigen den „Tribut an die Welt des Luxus", den Bulgari bei der Gestaltung des Hotels als Leitmotiv wählte. Das sinnliche Spa mit Goldmosaik-Pool und grün schimmerndem Hammam sollte sich kein Gast entgehen lassen – die Beautyanwendungen und Massagen mit duftenden Essenzen symbolisieren la dolce vita in seiner schönsten Form. Dem italienischen Lebensgefühl haben sich auch die Lounge und das Restaurant mit nationaler Küche verschrieben. Durch hohe Panoramafenster blickt man während des Essens direkt ins Grüne – an warmen Tagen wird zudem die traumhafte Terrasse geöffnet.

01 | The pool and hammam are waiting to pamper you in the purist spa.

Im puristischen Spa verwöhnen Pool und Hammam.

02 | The botanical gardens border directly on the private park.
Direkt an den Privatpark grenzt der Botanische Garten.

03 | The rooms display deluxe Italian design.
Die Zimmer zeigen italienisches Design de luxe.

03

byblos art hotel villa amista | verona . italy

DESIGN: Alessandro Mendini

Gnarled olive trees, splashing fountains, and spacious parks: The richly adorned Venetian villa from the 15th Century that now houses the Byblos Art Hotel Villa Amistà lies at the center of romantic gardens. From the outside, the luxury hotel near Verona looks like a feudal estate from the Baroque period. This makes the interior even more surprising: Nude photographs by artist Vanessa Beecroft are displayed between stucco tendrils in the reception hall, sculptures by Anish Kapoor stand on the intarsia parquet, and the comic-like figurines of the Japanese Takashi Murakami pop up in front of original frescos. The novel design comes from star architect Alessandro Mendini. With a great love of detail, he had all of the stylish stucco designs and ceiling frescos in the lobby, in all of the suites, and in the restaurant restored, combining them with contemporary art and brightly colored designer furniture. For example, vibrant orange-colored seating islands invite visitors to an aperitif in Peter's Bar. The unique wellness area with a Roman bathing vault and king-size outdoor pool is also glamorous and playful. The spa treatments like hydrotherapy and tropical showers are based on the knowledge of traditional Chinese methods in which the focus is on the unity of body, mind, and soul.

Knorrige Olivenbäume, plätschernde Springbrunnen, weitläufige Parkanlagen: Inmitten romantischer Gärten liegt die reich verzierte venezianische Villa aus dem 15. Jahrhundert, die heute das Byblos Art Hotel Villa Amistà beherbergt. Von Außen wirkt das Luxushotel nahe Verona wie ein feudales Anwesen aus der Barockzeit. Um so mehr überrascht das Interieur: Im Empfangssaal hängen Aktfotografien der Künstlerin Vanessa Beecroft zwischen Stuckranken, Skulpturen von Anish Kapoor stehen auf Intarsienparkett und die comicartigen Figurinen des Japaners Takashi Murakami tauchen vor original Fresken auf. Die originelle Gestaltung stammt von dem Stararchitekten Alessandro Mendini. Mit viel Liebe zum Detail ließ er die stilvollen Stukkaturen und Deckenfresken in der Lobby, in allen Suiten und im Restaurant restaurieren und kombinierte sie mit zeitgenössischer Kunst und grellfarbigen Designermöbeln. Leuchtend orangefarbene Sitzinseln laden beispielsweise in „Peter's Bar" zum Aperitif ein. Ebenfalls glamourös-verspielt ist der einzigartige Wellnessbereich mit römischem Badegewölbe und King-Size Außenpool. Die Spa-Behandlungen wie Hydrotherapie und Tropenduschen basieren auf Erkenntnissen traditioneller chinesischer Heilmethoden, bei denen die Einheit von Körper, Geist und Seele im Mittelpunkt steht.

01 | Playground of the styles: Splendid Murano glass chandeliers, candy-colored designer furniture, and the photo art of Vanessa Beecroft.

Spielplatz der Stile: Prächtige Murano Glaslüster, bonbonbunte Designermöbel und Fotokunst von Vanessa Beecroft.

02 | Mosaics meet frescos and chains of neon lights in the pool vault.

Im Poolgewölbe treffen Mosaiken auf Fresken und Neonlichterketten.

03 | Orange-colored seating islands and tables by Eero Saarinen in Peter's Bar.

Orangefarbene Sitzinseln und Tische von Eero Saarinen in Peter's Bar.

04 | Pool bar under a tent roof with Oriental flair.

Poolbar unter einem orientalisch anmutendem Zeltdach.

04

05

05 | Unique mix of styles: A side table by the Finnish designer Aero Aarnio in front of an opulent fireplace.

Einzigartiger Stilmix: Ein Beistelltisch des finnischen Designers Aero Aarnio vor einem opulenten Kamin.

le méridien lav | split . croatia

DESIGN: Lorenzo Bellini

Croatia reaches for the stars. The first Le Méridien Hotel of the country has opened on the stretch of the Podstrana coast, which is lined with stone-pine forests and tamarisk bushes. The luxury project is a success: The elegant look of the suites was created by the Italian designer Lorenzo Bellini with warm earth tones, tastefully patterned wallpaper, and desks of dark woods. The prizewinning designer Jim Nicolay from Hawaii laid out the gardens that stretch down to the ocean and one of the most beautiful beaches of the Adriatic. The Art Café, where paintings of Croatian artists are presented, is situated here between the royal palms. The terrace directly next door offers an amazing view of Split—the cultural metropolis of Dalmatia—and the surrounding islands of Braè, Korcula, Hvar, and Vis. These islands can be reached by ferry in just under two hours. The indoor swimming pool and spa with wall mosaics in Roman style, saunas, steam baths, and meditation room are in a pavilion with glass walls on all sides. The upper two gallery floors have steppers and treadmills for fitness with a view of the ocean. The outside pool blends with the ocean into a blue glittering expanse. And if you arrive in your own yacht, you can dock in the hotel's private marina.

Kroatien greift nach Sternen. Am Küstenstreifen Podstrana, gesäumt von Pininenwäldern und Tamariskensträuchern, eröffnete das erste Le Méridien Hotel des Landes. Das Luxusprojekt ist gelungen: Den eleganten Look der Suiten kreierte der italienische Designer Lorenzo Bellini mit warmen Erdtönen, dezent gemusterten Tapeten und Schreibtischen aus dunklen Hölzern. Der preisgekrönte Designer Jim Nicolay aus Hawaii gestaltete die Gärten, die sich bis zum Meer und zu einem der schönsten Strände der Adria erstrecken. Zwischen Königspalmen liegt hier das beliebte „Art Café", wo Malereien kroatischer Künstler präsentiert werden. Gleich nebenan bietet sich von der Terrasse aus eine umwerfende Aussicht auf Split, die kulturelle Metropole Dalmatiens, und auf die umliegenden Inseln Braè, Korcula, Hvar und Vis, die man mit der Fähre in knapp zwei Stunden erreicht. In einem rundum verglasten Pavillon liegen Hallenbad und Spa mit Wandmosaiken im römischen Stil, Saunen, Dampfbädern und Meditationsraum. Auf zwei Galerieetagen darüber stehen Stepper und Laufbänder zur Fitness mit Blick auf das Meer bereit. Der Außenpool verbindet sich mit dem Meer zu einer blau glitzernden Einheit. Und wer mit der eigenen Yacht anreist, kann in der privaten Marina des Hotels anlegen.

01 | Designed like a Roman bath: The resting area of mosaic stones in the spa.
Gestaltet wie ein römisches Bad: die Liegewiese aus Mosaikstei-nen im Spa.

02 | The glass-wall galleries around the pool offer fabulous views of the Adriatic coast.

Rund um den Pool bieten verglaste Galerien traumhafte Ausblicke auf die Adriaküste.

semiramis | athens . greece

DESIGN: Karim Rashid

Once you leave the hustle and bustle of downtown behind you in the taxi, you reach the green suburb of Kifissa at 1,115 feet above sea level. The quarter, popular with designers and artists because of its many boutiques, hip restaurants, and cafés, offers a perfect setting for the unique design hotel Semiramis. The Egyptian designer Karim Rashid—internationally renowned for his organically formed creations in vivid colors—has let his creativity run wild here—down to the smallest luxury detail: Each suite offers a cordless headphone for the personal DVD/CD player. Rashid designed the furniture and artwork for the entire hotel, as well as the backdrop for the sundeck—a water-colored wall mosaic. The organically formed infinity pool, the hammam, and the fitness zone with a personal trainer are the highlights in the beauty area of the hotel. This is especially interesting for the night owls who seek relaxation after excursions to the clubs of Athens. If you prefer a romantic dinner, secure a spot on the pool terrace beneath the pastel-colored sunshades. Everything is drenched in a pale pink light here during the twilight hour.

Nachdem man im Taxi die quirlige Innenstadt hinter sich gelassen hat, erreicht man 340 Meter oberhalb des Meeresspiegels den grünen Vorort Kifissa. Das bei Designern und Künstlern beliebte Viertel mit seinen vielen Boutiquen, Szenerestaurants und Cafes bietet eine perfekte Umgebung für das einzigartige Designhotel Semiramis. Der ägyptische Designer Karim Rashid, weltweit bekannt für seine organisch geformten Entwürfe in Knallfarben, hat hier seiner Kreativität freien Lauf gelassen – bis ins kleinste Luxusdetail: In jeder Suite liegen schnurlose Kopfhörer für den eigenen DVD/CD-Player bereit. Rashid entwarf die Möbel und Kunstwerke des gesamten Hotels ebenso wie die Kulisse für das Sonnendeck, ein wasserfarbenes Wandmosaik. Der organisch geformte Infinity-Pool, das Hammam und der Fitnessbereich mit Personal Trainer sind Highlights im Beautybereich des Hotels, vor allem für Nachtschwärmer, die nach Ausflügen in die Athener Clubs Entspannung suchen. Wer ein romantisches Abendessen bevorzugt, sollte sich einen Platz auf der Poolterrasse unter den pastellfarbenen Sonnenschirmen sichern, die zur Dämmerstunde in blass rosafarbenes Licht getaucht wird.

01 | Pastel-colored like soft ice cream: Pool and terrace as a total work of art.

Pastellfarben wie Softeis: Pool und Terrasse als Gesamtkunstwerk.

02

02 | The sunshine-yellow Plexiglas arch leads to the sofa lounge.

Der sonnengelbe Plexiglasbogen führt in die Sofalounge.

03 | Karim Rashid has also proved his talent in designing the lighting.

Auch beim Lichtdesign hat Karim Rashid sein Talent bewiesen.

04 | The bar: Funky colors like the Ruby Violet cocktail.

Die Bar: Verrückte Farben wie im Cocktail Ruby Violet.

05 | Furniture without corners and edges are the trademarks of Karim Rashid.

Möbel ohne Ecken und Kanten sind Markenzeichen von Karim Rashid.

06 | Time-out for pink and lilac: The suites are dominated by radiant white.

Auszeit für Pink und Lila: In den Suiten dominiert strahlendes Weiß.

07 | High-tech luxury and sun terrace—both are combined at Semiramis.

Hightech-Luxus und Sonnenterrasse – im Semiramis wird beides vereint.

blue palace resort & spa | crete . greece

DESIGN: Team around Angelos Angelopoulos, 3 SK Stylianides, Costantza Sbokou, Maria Vafiadi

Its breathtaking view of the Greek Aegean alone is what makes the Blue Palace Resort & Spa so appealing. The luxurious resort across from the enchanted island of Spinalonga has 142 (!) private infinity pools in a bright cobalt blue that competes with the color of the Mediterranean and the sky. Relaxation is on the agenda here—beneath the Mediterranean sun, in the shade of the palm and olive trees, in the stylishly designed bungalows, suites, and villas or at the Elounda Spa, which has been distinguished as one of the best spas in Greece. Many treatments are based on Cretan products such as fragrant herbs and golden olive oil—a massage in the open-air pavilion promises luxury for all of the senses. The thalassic therapies, which use the power of the ocean for health and well-being, are also excellent. Besides the awarded Mediterranean Gourmet Restaurant L'Orangerie, four more restaurants serve seasonally fresh Greek, Italian, and Asian cuisine; be sure to enjoy the nightcap after dinner outside the stars. Honeymooners also appreciate the idyllic flair of the resort—the hotel's own Romantic Department conjures up unforgettable honeymoons.

Allein schon der atemberaubende Blick auf die Griechische Ägäis macht das Blue Palace Resort & Spa so reizvoll. Das luxuriöse Resort gegenüber der verwunschenen Insel Spinalonga besitzt 142 (!) private Infinity Pools, deren leuchtendes Kobaltblau dem Mittelmeer und Himmel Konkurrenz machen. Entspannung ist hier Programm – unter mediterraner Sonne, im Schatten von Palmen und Olivenbäumen, in den stilvoll designten Bungalows, Suiten und Villen oder im Elounda Spa, das als bestes Spa Griechenlands ausgezeichnet wurde. Viele Anwendungen basieren auf kretischen Produkten wie duftenden Kräutern und goldglänzendem Olivenöl – eine Massage im Open-air Pavillon verspricht Luxus für alle Sinne. Auch die Thalassotherapien, die die Kraft des Ozeans für Gesundheit und Wohlbefinden nutzen, sind hervorragend. Neben dem mediterranen Gourmet-Restaurant L'Orangerie, servieren vier weitere Restaurants saisonfrische griechische, italienische und asiatische Küche; den Schlummertrunk nach dem Dinner sollte man unbedingt draußen unter den Sternen genießen. Das idyllische Flair des Resorts schätzen übrigens auch Honeymooner – das hauseigene „Romantic Department" zaubert unvergessliche Flitterwochen.

01 | The architecture combines Greek tradition and modern trends.
Die Architektur verbindet griechische Tradition und Moderne.

02 | The Villa Almyra presents an open view of the ocean.

Die Villa Almyra eröffnet unverstellte Blicke aufs Meer.

03 | The pool and the sea seem to merge seamlessly.

Der Pool und das Meer scheinen eins zu werden.

04 | Unique interior design: Master Bedroom of Villa Almyra.

Einzigartiges Interieur: Schlafzimmer der Villa Almyra.

04

belvedere | mykonos . greece

DESIGN: Rockwell Group

The location of this old manor house is ideal. It dominates the scenery on a little hill in the town of Chora, just a few minutes away from the boutiques and bars with a select clientele almost throughout the entire year. This luxurious hotel has always been in the hands of the Ioanidis family. They have long been established and not connected with any hotel chain. In keeping with these traditions, the house represents a personal atmosphere in which people know each other because many visitors return time and again. 41 rooms are arranged in six complexes around a spacious pool in the courtyard. Six suites, as well as an extremely roomy VIP accommodation, complete the offer. The architecture of this straightforward complex is characterized by the style of the island: white, rambling cubes, together with rounded walls and airy verandas sporting simple wooden roofs that are also painted white. Sail-like sheets protect against too much light. No room looks like any of the others and each one has an individual touch. But what they all have in common is that they are bright and airy, offering many areas for relaxation. However, the rooms with their fabulous views are not the only places for well-being. The spa of the Belvedere offers guests a fitness studio, a jacuzzi, and a steam bath, as well as soothing skin-care treatments.

Ideal ist die Lage dieses alten Herrenhauses. Es thront auf einer Anhöhe des Ortes Chora, nur wenige Minuten entfernt von den Boutiquen und Bars, durch die fast ganzjährig eine ausgesuchte Klientel streift. Von je her befindet sich diese luxuriöse Adresse in den Händen der Familie Ioanidis. Sie ist alteingesessen und mit keiner Hotelkette verbunden. Entsprechend steht das Haus für eine persönliche Atmosphäre, in der man sich kennt, denn viele Besucher kehren immer wieder. 41 Zimmer in sechs Komplexen sind um einen ausgedehnten Pool im Hof angelegt. Sechs Suiten sowie eine überaus geräumige VIP-Unterkunft vervollständigen das Angebot. Die Architektur dieser überschaubaren Anlage ist geprägt vom Stil der Insel: weiße, in sich verwinkelte Kuben, dazu abgerundetes Mauerwerk und luftige Veranden mit einfachen, ebenfalls weiß gestrichenen Holzdächern. Segelartige Tücher schützen vor Lichteinfall. Kein Raum gleicht dem anderen, jeder vermittelt eine individuelle Note. Allen ist aber gemeinsam, dass sie hell und luftig sind und zahlreiche Plätze zum Ausruhen bieten. Doch nicht nur in den Zimmern mit märchenhaftem Ausblick kann man es sich gut gehen lassen. Im Spa des Belvedere warten ein Fitness-Studio, ein Jacuzzi und ein Dampfbad ebenso wie wohltuende Pflege-Anwendungen auf die Gäste.

01 | There are a total of 41 rooms and six suites, some of which have upholstered terraces and sails that provide shade.

Insgesamt gibt es 41 Zimmer und sechs Suiten, einige davon mit gepolsterten Terrassen und schattenspendenden Segeln.

02 | The view of Myconos makes the complex one of the most popular places to live on the island.

Ein solcher Blick über Mykonos macht die Anlage zu einem der begehrtesten Wohnplätze auf der Insel.

03 | Cozy beds and sofas give the interior furnishings their character.

Gemütliche Betten und Sofas prägen die Inneneinrichtung.

04 | You can have stylish meals and spend the evening in the restaurant with its attached Belvedere Bar.

Stilvoll essen und den Abend verbringen kann man im Restaurant mit angeschlossener Belvedere Bar.

04

mykonos theoxenia | mykonos . greece

DESIGN: Yiannis Tsimas, Angelos Angelopoulos

Theoxenia Hotel takes you back to the Swinging Sixties. The legendary hotel on Myconos was one of the most fashionable accomodations of the Aegaen more than forty years ago. But the plaster began to crumble and the hotel - situated directly next to the famous typical windmills with their whitewashed walls and reed-thatched roofs that look like pointed caps—got a modern facelift. The interior designers Angelos Angelopoulos and Yiannis Tsimas have renewed the traditional white-blue palette of colors with fresh lemon-yellow, turquoise, and orange. The armchairs and sofas were given covers with retro patterns. The team placed azure chairs created by the Spanish designer Patricia Urquiola in front of the thick natural-stone walls, an architectural feature of the Cyclades. The white chairs at the pool, positioned between the stone pines and the palm trees, are the work of designer Ron Adler. The bhealthy club spa entices visitors with massages and fitness courses. Those who prefer to have the ocean breeze blow around them can indulge in an al-fresco massage at one of the four-poster beds of the pool veranda. Two bars called Breeze In and Breeze Out offer exotic drinks and snacks—time for conscious enjoyment: The names alone promise relaxation.

In die Swinging Sixties fühlt man sich im Theoxenia Hotel zurückversetzt. Vor über vierzig Jahren gehörte das legendäre Hotel auf Mykonos zu einem der schicksten Unterkünfte der Ägäis. Doch der Putz fing an zu bröckeln und so bekam das Hotel, das direkt neben den berühmten, landestypischen Windmühlen mit ihren getünchten Mauern und reetgedeckten Zipfelmützendächern liegt, ein modernes Facelifting. Die Interieurdesigner Angelos Angelopoulos und Yiannis Tsimas haben die traditionell weiß-blaue Farbpalette mit frischem Zitronengelb, Türkis und Orange aufgefrischt. Sessel und Sofas bekamen Bezüge mit Retromustern und vor die dicken Natursteinmauern, einem Architekturmerkmal der Kykladen, platzierte das Team azurblaue Stühle, entworfen von der spanischen Designerin Patricia Urquiola. Der Gestalter Ron Adler entwarf die weißen Stühle am Pool, der zwischen Pinien- und Palmen angelegt wurde. Mit Massagen und Fitnessparkours lockt der „bhealthy club spa". Wer sich lieber die Meeresbrise um die Nase wehen lassen möchte, der gönnt sich eine „al fresco"-Massage auf einem der Himmelbetten auf der Pool-Veranda. Zu exotischen Drinks und Snacks laden zwei Bars genannt „Breeze In" und „Breeze Out" ein – bewußt genießen: allein die Namen versprechen schon Entspannung.

01 | Only the silhouettes of windmills can be recognized just after sunset.

Kurz nach Sonnenuntergang sind nur noch die Silhouetten der Windmühlen zu erkennen.

02 | Homage to the Sixties: Blue glazed vases, rocking armchairs, and graphic art in the lobby.

Hommage an die Sixties: Blaulasierte Vasen, Schaukelsessel und grafische Kunst in der Lobby.

03 | Instead of the country's typical blue-white, a strong tomato red is used here.

Statt landestypischem Blau-Weiß kommt kräftiges Tomatenrot zum Einsatz.

04 | Turquoise walls suggest the close proximinty to the Aegaen Sea.

Türkisfarbene Wände erinnern an die unmittelbare Nähe zum Ägäischen Meer.

03 04

almyra | paphos . cyprus

DESIGN: Joëlle Pléot, Tristan Auer

Converting existing buildings into design hotels usually means compromises and results that are never completely satisfactory. But there is no rule without an exception: The Almyra—created from the Paphos Beach Hotel on Cyprus after two years of renovation—is an establishment that is worth seeing. Much white and pastel, clear lines, and high-quality materials provide a contemporary Greek look. The Kyma Signature Suites directly on the ocean offer fantastic wide, open living and sleeping areas, as well as a 144 square feet roof terrace that is almost as large as the suite itself and reveals breathtaking views. Lit by candles in the evening, this is the perfect place for a Japanese-Mediterranean Omakase menu—the translation of which is something like "trust the cook". These culinary surprises can also be ordered at the al fresco Notios Restaurant (the hotel offers three additional outlets). The wellness plan includes aromatherapy and yoga, as well as acupuncture. And parents can enjoy all of the treatments in peace and quiet: Thanks to the Baby Go Lightly program, Almyra is one of the most family-friendly hotels in Greece.

Bestehende Bauten in Designhotels zu verwandeln, bedeutet normalerweise Kompromisse und Ergebnisse, die nie ganz zufriedenstellen. Doch keine Regel ohne Ausnahme: Das Almyra – nach zweijähriger Renovierung aus dem Paphos Beach Hotel auf Zypern entstanden – ist eine Adresse, die sich sehen lassen kann. Viel Weiß und Pastell, klare Linien und hochwertige Materialien sorgen für einen zeitgemäßen griechischen Look. Die Kyma Signature Suiten direkt am Meer bieten traumhaft weite und offene Wohn- und Schlafbereiche sowie eine Dachterrasse, die mit 44 Quadratmetern nochmals fast so groß wie die Suite selbst ist und atemberaubende Aussichten eröffnet. Abends von Kerzen beleuchtet, ist sie der perfekte Platz für ein japanisch-mediterranes „Omakase"-Menü – was übersetzt soviel bedeutet wie „Vertraue dem Koch". Diese kulinarischen Überraschungen kann man auch im Al fresco Restaurant „Notios" bestellen (zudem bietet das Hotel noch drei weitere Outlets). Auf dem Wellnessplan steht neben Aromatherapie und Yoga auch Akupunktur. – Eltern können alle Anwendungen übrigens ganz in Ruhe genießen: Dank des „Baby Go Lightly"-Programms gehört das Almyra zu den familienfreundlichsten Häusern Griechenlands.

01 | Airy and bathed in light: Helios Lounge of the Almyra.

Luftig und lichtdurchflutet: Die Helios Lounge des Almyra.

02 | Blue and white: Classic Greek colors in the rooms.

Blau und weiß: klassisch griechische Farben in den Zimmern.

03 | A touch of Asia: Comfortable loungers by the pool.
Asiatisch angehaucht: Ruheliegen am Pool.

04 | Favorite spots: Roof terraces of the Kyma Suites.
Lieblingsplätze: die Dachterrassen der Kyma-Suiten.

adam & eve | antalya/belek . turkey

DESIGN: Eren Talu

The ultramodern Adam & Eve goes far beyond the conventional dimensions: A turquoise-colored pool that is twice as long as an Olympic swimming pool runs parallel to the isolated sand beach on the coast in Belek near Antalaya. The guests enjoy the sundowner at a 288-foot bar. And each room is a postmodern work of art in itself with its own mini-spa and whirlpool. Idyllic hideaways are the three Turkish hammams, saunas, and solariums. You can book stone and thalassic therapies, Thai massages by flickering candlelight, and algae rejuvenation treatments in the massage rooms or spend a romantic evening with the partner in the Couple Suite where both of you can relax together. In the white rooms, the walls with mirrors extending from the floor to the ceiling reflect the Mediterranean. The secret hiding place of the night owls is the night pool, which is concealed in the middle of a stone-pine forest. Adam & Eve naturally also has its own hotel "angel". The personal butler anticipates every wish from the eyes of the vacationing guests: organize a birthday party, find a babysitter, create a surprise dinner—everything is possible.

Das ultramoderne Adam & Eve sprengt herkömmliche Dimensionen: Parallel zum einsamen Sandstrand an der Küste in Belek nahe Antalaya erstreckt sich ein türkisfarbener Pool, der doppelt so lang ist wie ein Olympia-Schwimmbecken. Den Sundowner genießen die Gäste an einer 88 Meter langen Bar. Und jedes Zimmer ist ein postmodernes Kunstwerk für sich mit eigenem Mini-Spa und Whirlpool. Idyllische Hideaways sind die drei türkischen Hammams, Saunen und Solarien. In den Massageräumen kann man Stone- und Thalasso-Therapien, Thai-Massagen bei flackerndem Kerzenlicht und Algenverjüngungskuren buchen oder mit dem Partner einen romantischen Abend in der „Couple Suite" verbringen, in der man zu Zweit entspannen kann. In den weißen Zimmern reflektieren die vom Boden bis zur Decke verspiegelten Wände das Mittelmeer. Geheimes Versteck der Nachtschwärmer ist der Night-Pool, der verborgen inmitten eines Pinienwaldes liegt. Natürlich hat das Adam & Eve auch einen hoteleigenen „Engel". Der persönliche Butler liest einem jeden Urlaubswunsch von den Augen ab: Geburtstagsparty organisieren, Babysitten, Überraschungsdinner – alles ist möglich.

01 | Shining, shimmering surfaces from the floor to the ceiling make the pool an ultramodern bathing landscape.

Spiegelblanke, schimmernde Oberflächen vom Boden bis zur Decke machen den Pool zur ultramodernen Badelandschaft.

02 | Brightness and transparency ensure a vacation mood.

Helligkeit und Transparenz sorgen für Urlaubsstimmung.

03 | Mirrored walls enlarge the spa into infinity.

Verspiegelte Wände vergrößern den Spa ins Unendliche.

04 | The rushing of the waves becomes the vacation melody during the day and night.

Das Rauschen der Wellen wird bei Tag und Nacht zur Urlaubsmelodie.

ev | bodrum . turkey

DESIGN: Eren Talu

The ultramodern residences of the EV hotel look like eight gigantic steps toward heaven. The recidences, up to 200 square feet in size, are distributed across a hill with an unrestricted view of peninsula, inlets, and capes running through Turkbuku Bay. The Turkish architect and interior designer Eren Talu has created a radically reduced design here—but without renouncing comfort. The geometric architecture with dazzling white, sharp contours is intended as a strong contrast to the undulating foothills of the Taurus Mountains in the hinterland. The cool color motif is also continued in the apartments: Light bed linens and sofas have a calming effect and simultaneously let positive energies flow. Large mirrors convey a sense of an endless expanse. The only splashes of color in the purist domicile are pink vases and storm lanterns. The modern bungalow facility has a wellness landscape with lawns, massage rooms, saunas, fitness areas, and eight swimming pools for variety. A short walk leads to a private beach with pebbles. And a jacuzzi bubbles in each of the bathrooms by request—at any time of the day or night. This is the service motto of the hotel: whatever and whenever.

Wie acht gigantische Treppenstufen in Richtung Himmel wirken die ultramodernen Bungalows des EV-Hotels. Die bis zu 185 Quadratmeter großen Apartments verteilen sich über einen Hügel mit freiem Blick auf die von Halbinseln, Buchten und Kaps durchzogene Türkbükü Bucht. Der türkische Architekt and Interieurdesigner Eren Talu hat hier radikal reduziertes Design geschaffen – ohne auf Komfort zu verzichten. Die geometrische Architektur mit blendend weißen, scharfen Konturen soll einen starken Kontrast zu den welligen Ausläufern des Taurusgebirges im Hinterland bilden. Das coole Farbmotiv setzt sich auch in den Apartments fort: Helle Leinenbettwäsche und Sofas beruhigen und lassen zugleich positive Energien fließen. Große Spiegel vermitteln ein Gefühl unendlicher Weite. Die einzigen Farbtupfer in dem puristischen Domizil sind rosarote Vasen und Windlichter. Rund um die moderne Bungalowanlage sorgt eine Wellnesslandschaft mit Rasenflächen, Massageräumen, Sauna, Fitnessareal und acht Swimmingpools für Abwechslung. Ein kurzer Spaziergang führt zu einem kieseligen Privatstrand. Und in jedem Badezimmer sprudelt auf Wunsch ein Jacuzzi – zu jeder Tages- und Nachtzeit. Denn das Sevicemotto des Hotels lautet: Was auch immer, wann auch immer.

01 | Stairway to heaven: The white residences of the hotel are located high above Turkbuku Bay.

Himmelsleiter: die weißen Bungalows des Hotels liegen hoch über der Türkbükü Bucht.

02

03

04

05

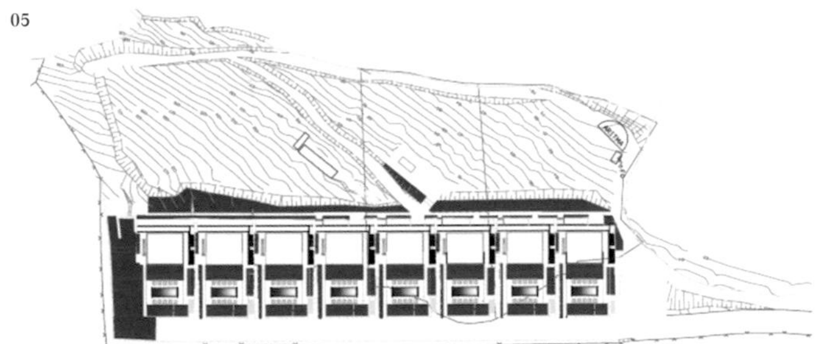

02 | Red flowers and a few lilac storm lights are the only dashes of color in the pure white interior.

Rote Blüten und ein paar lilafarbene Windlichter sind die einzigen Farbkleckse im reinweißen Interieur.

03 | Big mirrors make the room infinitely large.

Große Spiegel vergrößern den Raum ins Unendliche.

04 | Luxury lounging area on the roof terrace with a view of the bay's peninsula.

Luxus-Liegeplatz auf der Dachterrasse mit Aussicht auf die Halbinseln der Bucht.

05 | Plan.

Plan.

hotel index

Country / Location		Address	Information	Architecture & Design	Page
Portugal	Madeira	Choupana Hills Resort & Spa Travessa do Largo da Choupana 9060-348 Funchal Portugal www.choupanahills.com	opened 2002 58 deluxe rooms, 4 suites with jacuzzi. Restaurant, bars, lounge, fitness- and spa center with Turkish steam bath, sauna, heated indoor pool with jet massage and jacuzzi effect and heated outdoor lagoon pool, 2 golf courses nearby. Nestled on the verdant hillside of Funchal.	Michel de Camaret Didier Lefort	8
Portugal	Madeira	Estalagem da Ponta do Sol Quinta da Rochinha 9360-121 Ponta do Sol Portugal www.pontadosol.com	opened 2001 54 guestrooms with balcony and seaview. Restaurant, bar, poolside snack bar and café, 1 indoor pool, 1 outdoor pool, steam bath, jacuzzi and gym. Situated on the south coast of Madeira. 20-minute ride from Funchal.	Tiago Oliveira Carvalho Araujo	12
Spain	Barcelona	H 1898 La Rambla, 109 (Entrance via Carrer Pintor Fortuny) 08002 Barcelona, Spain www.nnhotels.com	opened 2005 169 rooms and suites with private pool and gardens, 5 conference rooms, business centre with free ADSL or WLAN internet access, restaurants, bars, cafés, library, gym, solarium, spa with steam rooms, sauna, massage, indoor and outdoor pool. Located at La Rambla, in the heart of Barcelona.	Rosa Roselló	16
Spain	Tarragona	Le Méridien RA Beach Hotel & Spa Avinguda Sanatori, 1 El Vendrell, 43880 Spain www.starwoodhotels.com	opened 2007 143 rooms, restaurants, piano-bar, 7,200 m² wellness area, thalassotherapy treatments, fitness, indoor and outdoor pool, private beach. Located on the Costa Daurada. 40-minute ride from Barcelona.	Espinet i Ubach Arquitectes	22
Spain	Mallorca	Hotel Maricel Carretera de Andratx, No. 11 07181 Ca's Català - Calvià Spain www.hospes.es	opened 2002 6 double rooms with mountain view, 14 double rooms with sea view, 4 double rooms with sea view and terrace, 4 suites with sea view and 1 suite with sea view and large terrace. Library, outdoor pool, wellness area with sauna, massages, fitness and private landing place. 15-minute ride from airport.	Hospes Design	26

hotel index

Country / Location		Address	Information	Architecture & Design	Page
Spain	Mallorca	Son Brull Hotel & Spa Carretera Palma- Pollensa MA 2200 Km 50 Pollensa 07460 Mallorca, Spain www.sonbrull.com	opened 2003 23 rooms, restaurant, bar, spa, sauna, Turkish steam room, jacuzzi, indoor and outdoor pool, tennis court. 5-minute ride from the village center of Pollença, 45-minute ride from airport.	Ignasi Forteza Sebastian Gamundí	32
France	Corsica	Casadelmar Route de Palombaggia BP 93 20538 Porto-Vecchio Cedex, South Corsica France www.casadelmar.fr	opened 2004 31 rooms and suites, restaurants, lounge bar, spa with 4 massage cabins, gym, hammam, relaxation rooms, heated outdoor pool, private beach and pier. Located near the Porto Vecchio bay. 25-minute ride from Figari International Airport.	Jean François Bodin Carole Marcellesi	36
France	Hagetmau	Hôtel des Lacs d'Halco Route de Cazalies 40700 Hagetmau France www.hotel-des-lacs-dhalco.com	opened 2001 24 rooms, restaurant La Dame du Lac, regular tasting sessions and indoor pool. At the Pyrenees, 60-minute ride from the Atlantic Ocean.	Eric Raffy	40
UK	Cowley	Cowley Manor Cowley near Cheltenham Gloucestershire Cowley GL 53 9NL United Kingdom www.cowleymanor.com	opened 2002 30 rooms, restaurant, spa area with sauna, steam bath, indoor and outdoor swimming pool and three lakes. 64 km from Oxford and 155 km from London.	De Matos Storey Ryan	44
UK	Chandler's Cross	The Grove Chandler's Cross, Hertfordshire, WD3 4TG United Kingdom www.thegrove.co.uk	opened 2003 212 rooms and 15 suites, 3 restaurants with bars and terraces. Sequoia Spa with pool, jacuzzi, sauna, vitality pool and treatment rooms, 18-hole-golf-course. Garden with pool, tennis courts and croquet lawn. 40-minute ride from central London, 30-minute ride from London Heathrow Airport.	Fox Linton Fitzroy Robinson	48

hotel index

Country / Location	Address	Information	Architecture & Design	Page
Finland Helsinki	Klaus K Bulevardi 2 00120 Helsinki Finland www.klauskhotel.com	opened 2005 135 rooms, 2 suites, 1 meeting room, 1 ball room, 3 restaurants, champagne bar, night club, spa, sauna and gym. Located in the heart of Helsinki. Less than 20 km from Helsinki International Airport.	SARC Architects (Antti-Matti Siikala, Sarlotta Narjos) Stylt Trampoli (Kasja Krause)	52
Germany Berlin	Hotel de Rome Behrenstraße 37 10117 Berlin Germany www.roccofortehotels.com	opened 2006 101 rooms, 32 junior suites, 13 suites, 5 meeting rooms, 1 ballroom, restaurant, spa with plunge pool, steam, sauna and relaxation area, gym and 20 m swimming pool. Located in the heart of Berlin. 17-minute ride from Tegel International Airport.	Tommaso Ziffer Olga Polizzi	56
Germany Berlin	Q! Knesebeckstraße 67 10623 Berlin Germany www.loock-hotels.com	opened 2004 72 rooms, 4 studios, 1 penthouse, restaurant, bar, spa area with sauna, vapour-bath, Japanese wash zone, massage and sandroom. 15-minute ride from Tegel International Airport.	Graft Architects	60
Germany Donaueschingen	Der Öschberghof Golfplatz 1 78166 Donaueschingen Germany www.oeschberghof.com	opened 1976, last renovation 2001 (hotel), 2006 (spa) 73 rooms and suites, 2 restaurants, bar, wellness area with whirlpool, sauna, indoor pool, and 2 golf courses. Located at the edge of the Black Forest, 125 km from Stuttgart, 90 km from Zurich.	Markus-Diedenhofen	66
Switzerland Arosa	Tschuggen Grand Hotel Sonnenbergstrasse 7050 Arosa Switzerland www.tschuggen.ch	opened 1929, last renovation 2007 98 rooms, 32 suites, 4 restaurants, bar, 5,000 m^2 spa area, sauna, jacuzzis, pools, medical wellness, 2 spa suites, indoor and outdoor pool. Located in the Swiss Alps, 170 km from Zurich.	Carlo Rampazzi (Hotel) Mario Botta (Spa)	70

hotel index

Country / Location	Address	Information	Architecture & Design	Page
Switzerland Geneva	La Réserve Genève Hotel & Spa Route de Lausanne 301 1293 Bellevue Switzerland www.lareserve.ch	reopened 2003 85 rooms, 17 suites, 3 restaurants, 2 bars, spa area with sauna, hammam, gym, indoor and outdoor pool, venezian transfer boat. Located at the shore of Lake Geneva. 10-minute ride from Geneva International Airport.	Patrice Reynaud Jacques Garcia	74
Switzerland Interlaken	Victoria-Jungfrau Grand Hotel & Spa Höheweg 41 3800 Interlaken Switzerland www.victoria-jungfrau.ch	opened 1865/1869, enhancement ESPA 2003 212 rooms, 1 gourmet restaurant La Terrasse, swiss restaurant Jungfrau Brasserie, La Pastateca, 2 bars, spa bar, spa with sauna, steam room, solaria, salt-water jacuzzi, swimming pool, fitness and tennis court. Located at the foot of "Jungfrau", "Mönch" and "Eiger". 2-hour ride from Zurich International Airport.	Wolfgang Behles Ernst Anderegg Jo Brinkmann	78
Switzerland Weggis	Park Hotel Weggis Hertensteinstrasse 34 6353 Weggis Switzerland www.phw.ch	new building opened 2007 34 rooms, 19 suites, restaurants, bars, vinotheque, wellness area with six 60 m² "spa cottages" and Asian bath temple, courtyard with Japanese garden. Located at the shore of the Lake of Lucerne. 45-minute ride from Zurich International Airport.	Vincenz Erni Aldoplan AG Vadian Metting van Rijn Pius Notter	82
Switzerland Vals	Therme Vals 7132 Vals Switzerland www.therme-vals.ch	opened 1970 (hotel), opened 1996 (therme) 140 rooms, 2 restaurants, thermal bath Vals with several indoor and outdoor pools. Located in the Vals valley. 2-hour ride from Zurich International Airport.	Peter Zumthor	86
Switzerland Zermatt	The Omnia Auf dem Fels 3920 Zermatt Switzerland www.the-omnia.com	opened 2006 18 rooms, 12 suites, restaurant, lounge bar, private club, wellness center with sauna, Turkish bath, massage, fitness, yoga, pilates, indoor and outdoor pool. Located in the heart of Zermatt. 3-hour ride from Geneva International Airport.	Ali Tayar	90

hotel index

Country / Location	Address	Information	Architecture & Design	Page
Austria Bezau	Hotel Post Brugg 35 6870 Bezau Austria www.hotelpostbezau.com	new building opened 1998, opened 2006 (spa) 50 rooms, 3 meeting rooms, Gault Millau awarded restaurant, beauty and wellness area, sauna, steam bath, jacuzzi, fitness, indoor pool, tennis court. 1½-hour ride from Zurich International Airport.	Oskar Leo Kaufmann Johannes Kaufmann	94
Austria Ischgl	Design Hotel Madlein 6561 Ischgl Austria www.madlein.com	new building opened 2000 80 rooms, restaurant, bar, lounge, zen garden, spa area with sauna, steam bath, indoor pool, outdoor sauna and outdoor whirlpool. 2½-hour ride from Zurich International Airport.	Sabine Mescherowsky Gregor Mescherowsky	98
Austria Langenlois	wine & spa resort LOISIUM Hotel Loisium Allee 2 3550 Langenlois Austria www.loisiumhotel.at	opened 2005 82 rooms and suites, restaurant, AVEDA wine spa, yoga, tai-chi, vinotherapy, sauna, fitness, 2 vintage relax lounges, aroma steam bath, sun-terrace and heated outdoor pool. 1-hour ride from Vienna International Airport.	Steven Holl	102
Austria Zell am See	Mavida Balance Hotel & Spa Kirchenweg 11 5700 Zell am See Austria www.mavida.at	opened 2005 47 rooms and suites, restaurant, bar, lounge, library, spa- and wellness area, 2 saunas, private spa suite, indoor pool, private floating pool, gym and 2 championship golf courses. Located just a few steps from the lake and the skiing area. 50-minute ride from Salzburg Airport.	Niki Szilagyi	106
Italy Lana	vigilius mountain resort Vigiljoch Mountain 39011 Lana Italy www.vigilius.it	opened 2003 35 rooms and 6 suites, 2 restaurants, wine cellar, bar, Mountain lounge, library, spa with sauna, steam bath, jacuzzi, indoor swimming pool. Located 1500 m above sea level, reachable only by cable car. 8 km from Merano.	Matteo Thun	110

hotel index

Country / Location	Address	Information	Architecture & Design	Page
Italy — Milan 	Bulgari Milan Via Privata Fratelli Gabba 7/b 20121 Milan Italy www.bulgarihotels.com	opened 2004 58 rooms and suites, restaurant, lounge, indoor pool, spa, hammam, fitness center and 4,000 m² private garden. Located in the heart of Milan, next to the Botanical garden.	Antonio Citterio and Partner	116
Italy — Verona 	Byblos Art Hotel Villa Amista Via Cedrare, 78 37029 Corrubbio di Negarine Italy www.byblosarthotel.com	opened 2005 49 rooms and 11 suites, restautants, bars, wine cellar, fitness, spa, sauna, indoor and outdoor pool. 7 km from the city center of Verona. 90-minute ride from Venice Marco Polo International Airport.	Alessandro Mendini	120
Croatia — Split 	Le Méridien Lav, Split Grljevacka, 2A 21312 Podstrana – Split Croatia www.starwoodspacollection.com	opened 2006 381 rooms and suites, 8 restaurants and bars, casino, spa with 8 treatment rooms, 1 deluxe room with water bed and a private pool, Roman baths, sauna, jacuzzi, adventure showers, outdoor and indoor pool. 8 km south of Split. 15-minute ride from Split International Airport.	Lorenzo Bellini	126
Greece — Athens 	Semiramis Charilaou Trikoupi 48 14562 Kefalari – Kifissia Greece www.semiramisathens.com	opened 2004 51 rooms, including 4 rooftop suites and 5 poolside bungalows, restaurant, bar, private party room, meeting rooms, gym, wellness center, hammam, outdoor pool. 20-minute ride from Athens International Airport.	Karim Rashid	130
Greece — Crete 	Blue Palace Resort & Spa 72053 Elounda Greece www.bluepalace.gr	opened 2003 251 rooms, 5 restaurants, 3 bars, spa, thalassotherapy, massages, gym, sauna, hammam, jacuzzi, 1 heated indoor pool, 2 outdoor pools with sea water, 1 outdoor pool with fresh water. Located on the northeast coast of Crete at the gulf of Elounda. 1-hour ride from the airport.	Team around Angelos Angelopoulos 3 SK Stylianides Costantza Sbokou Maria Vafiadi	136

hotel index

Country / Location	Address	Information	Architecture & Design	Page
Greece Mykonos	Belvedere School of Fine Arts District 84 600 Mykonos Greece www.belvederehotel.com	opened 1995 41 rooms, 6 suites, internet corner, CD and DVD library, sushi restaurant, snack and pool bar, sunset bar, 24 hours state of the art gym, spa facilities, outdoor pool. 5-minute walk from island´s center, five-minute ride to Mykonos Airport.	Rockwell Group	140
Greece Mykonos	Mykonos Theoxenia Kato Mili 84600 Mykonos Greece www.mykonostheoxenia.com	opened 2004 52 rooms and suites, gourmet restaurant The Plate, cocktail bar, gym, jacuzzi, massage-room, outdoor pool with pool bar, palm garden. 5-minute ride from the airport and port.	Yiannis Tsimas Angelos Angelopoulos	144
Cyprus Paphos	Almyra Poseidonos Avenue 8042 Paphos Cyprus www.thanoshotels.com	opened 2003 A newly designed spa opens 2008. 158 rooms, 4 restaurants, rooftop terraces, sauna, gym, aromatherapy, yoga, jacuzzi, 2 outdoor pools and tennis courts. Located 16 km from Paphos International Airport, 130 km from Larnaca International Airport.	Tristan Auer Joëlle Pléot	148
Turkey Antalya / Belek	Adam & Eve İskele Mevkii Belek Turkey www.adamevehotels.com	opened 2006 434 rooms, 29 suites and 24 villas, 8 restaurants, eden spa center, hammam, 2 private hammams, 2 saunas, solarium, massages, indoor pool, sports and golf. Located 30 km from Antalya.	Eren Talu	152
Turkey Bodrum	EV Turkbuku Bodrum Turkey www.evturkbuku.com	opened 2004 48 rooms with terrace, jacuzzi in all bathrooms, fitness area, sauna, 4 massage rooms, 8 heated private outdoor pools and beach. 40 km from Bodrum International Airport.	Eren Talu	156

architects & designers

photo credits

imprint

Bibliographic information published by the Deutsche Nationalbibliothek
The Deutsche Nationalbibliothek lists this publication in the Deutsche Nationalbibliografie; detailed bibliographic data are available in the Internet at http://dnb.d-nb.de.

ISBN: 978-3-89986-090-0

Second updated edition

Printed in Austria
by Vorarlberger Verlagsanstalt AG, Dornbirn

avedition GmbH
Königsallee 57 | 71638 Ludwigsburg | Germany
p +49-7141-1477391 | f +49-7141-1477399
www.avedition.com | contact@avedition.com

Further information and links at
www.bestdesigned.com
www.fusion-publishing.com

Team: Martin Nicholas Kunz (Editor), Patricia Massó (Editorial coordination), Hanna Martin (Editorial management), Mariel Marohn, Anne-Kathrin Meier (Editorial assistance), Katharina Feuer (Layout), Jan Hausberg, Martin Herterich (Imaging & prepress), Elke Roberta Buscher (Texts pp. 8, 12, 26, 40, 44, 82, 86, 94, 98, 110 and 140), Camilla Peus (Texts pp. 22, 52, 72, 90, 102, 106, 120, 126, 130, 144, 152 and 156), Anna Streubert (Introduction, Texts pp. 16, 32, 36, 48, 56, 60, 66, 70, 78, 116, 136 and 148), Alphagriese Fachübersetzungen, Dusseldorf (Translations)

Special thanks to Katilena Alpe, DK Associates | Dr. Anja Baumeister, Der Öschberghof | Gianluca Bertilaccio, Casadelmar | Li Boatwright, Cowley Manor | Ulrike Brandner-Lauter, wine & spa resort LOISIUM Hotel | Valérie Burnier, Victoria-Jungfrau | Francesco Cirillo, Byblos Art Hotel Villa Amista | Cindy Coutinho, Choupana Hills Resort & Spa | Laure Demen, Hôtel des Lacs d'Halco | Maria Diakaki, Belvedere | Sonja Dietrich,Therme Vals | André Diogo, Estalagem da Ponta do Sol | Selin Edali, EV | Teresa Forcada, H 1898 | Tea M. Franić, Le Méridien | Dr. Ruth Gamper, vigilius mountain resort | Claudia Heiss, Hotel de Rome | Christian Henninger, Tschuggen Grand Hotel | Claudia Hubberten, Son Brull Hotel & Spa | Claudia Juen, Design Hotel Madlein | Maria Kalognomou, Blue Palace Spa & Resort | Fiona Kendall, Thanos Hotels | Katja Köllner, Katja Koellner PR | Charlotte von Koenen, Blue Palace Resort & Spa | Anna Llorens, Le Méridien | Tala Majzoub, La Réserve Genève Hotel & Spa | Pasi Nakki, Klaus K | Eva-Maria Rabini, Bulgari Milan | Nicole Rohner, Park Hotel Weggis | Juan Segura, Maricel | Kian Shams-Dolatabadi, Q! | Despina Skeva, Semiramis | Adrian Stalder, stalderprojects sagl | Irene Teubner, Mavida Balance Hotel & Spa | Kathrine Walsh, The Grove | Melanie Wöhr, Hotel Post | Annalisa Zumthor, Therme Vals for their support.

Martin Nicholas Kunz
1957 born in Hollywood. Founder of fusion publishing creating content for architecture, design, travel, and lifestyle publications.

best designed wellness hotels:
asia pacific
americas
europe
africa & middle east

best designed:
beach hotels
honeymoon hotels
ecological hotels
affordable hotels
modular houses
outdoor living
hotel pools
flagship stores

best designed hotels:
asia pacific
americas
europe I (urban)
europe II (countryside)
swiss hotels

All books are released in German and English